50

THINGS YOU NEED
TO KNOW ABOUT

SATAN AND
DEMONS

50

THINGS YOU NEED TO KNOW ABOUT

SATAN AND DEMONS

MARK H. MUSKA

BETHANY HOUSE PUBLISHERS
a division of Baker Publishing Group
Minneapolis, Minnesota

© 2014 by Baker Publishing Group

Published by Bethany House Publishers
11400 Hampshire Avenue South
Bloomington, Minnesota 55438
www.bethanyhouse.com

Bethany House Publishers is a division of
Baker Publishing Group, Grand Rapids, Michigan

Printed in the United States of America

Library of Congress Cataloging-in-Publication Data
Muska, Mark H.
    50 things you need to know about Satan and demons / Mark H. Muska.
      pages cm
    Includes bibliographical references.
    Summary: "Bible professor gives short, clear answers to the most-asked questions about Satan and demons, revealing what the Bible does and doesn't say"— Provided by publisher.
    ISBN 978-0-7642-1234-5 (pbk. : alk. paper)
    1. Devil—Christianity—Miscellanea. 2. Demonology—Miscellanea.
3. Spiritual warfare—Miscellanea. I. Title. II. Title: Fifty things you need to know about Satan and demons.
BT982.M87 2014
235'.4—dc23
                                  2014031620

Cover design by LOOK Design Studio

14 15 16 17 18 19 20   7 6 5 4 3 2 1

Contents

Introduction

Of all the subjects related to Christianity, there isn't one quite like Satan and the demons. Almost everyone has heard about them. Most people believe in evil spirits. We think that we know quite a bit about them, too. The subject is scary, but intriguing. We are drawn to these evil powers by some strange magnetism. We also dread the thought of the devil on the loose, terrorizing the planet.

What most people believe about evil spirits is not so much based on what the handbook for Christianity—the Bible—says about demons. Our beliefs come largely from a long history of superstition, hearsay, folklore, and popular entertainment.

This study is based on the conviction that the Bible is our one reliable source of truth about the devil. We are going to look at what the Scriptures say about Satan, demons, spiritual warfare, and the occult. We won't ignore all of the folklore, but will test the stories against biblical truth.

Be prepared, however, for some disappointment if you think that all of your questions are going to be answered. Many times the Bible does not address our inquiries with the detail that we would like. But we will find ourselves hopelessly tangled in all of the folklore if we wander from the Scriptures. We will be helpless to discern the truth about Satan from all of the hype. Serious study about a formidable enemy will fall victim to sensationalism.

So strap yourself in and get ready for an informative and profitable ride through the scary world of Satan, demons, and the occult.

1 Who is Satan?

What if I told you about a person who, without you even being aware of it, is your mortal enemy? This person is very powerful, he has many allies gathered to fight with him against you, and he is evil to the core. He is crafty and relentlessly committed to your destruction. And to top things off, when he wants to, he acts without being seen or heard.

Do you want to learn more about this enemy? Are you interested in taking steps to protect yourself and your loved ones from this person's attacks?

This enemy is the devil. His name is Satan.

Who is Satan? The answer to that question is harder than you may think. Stories about Satan have circulated through the human race for thousands of years. Many are exaggerations, superstitions, or just plain lies about him. And he seems to be happy to contribute to the confusion! But what is the truth about Satan?

Thankfully, there is a reliable source of information. It is the Bible. We can learn a great deal about Satan from examining the pages of the Christian Scriptures. A good place to start is the first time that Satan appears in the Bible, in the book of Genesis. We discover several things about Satan.

> Now the serpent was more crafty than any of the wild animals the Lord God had made. He said to the woman [Eve], "Did God really say, 'You must not eat from any tree in the garden [of Eden]'?"

The woman said to the serpent, "We may eat fruit from the trees in the garden, but God did say, 'You must not eat fruit from the tree that is in the middle of the garden, and you must not touch it, or you will die.'"

"You will not certainly die," the serpent said to the woman. "For God knows that when you eat from it your eyes will be opened, and you will be like God, knowing good and evil."

Genesis 3:1–5

First, Satan chose to appear to Eve in disguise as an animal, a serpent. But Satan is not an animal; he spoke to Eve with intelligence. He has the ability to think and to make choices like a person.

Satan is also described as "crafty." He is cunning and shrewd. He was set on deceiving Eve.

- Satan misrepresented what God had said to Adam and Eve. God did not forbid them from eating from all the trees in the Garden of Eden. Just one tree was off-limits.

- He challenged directly what God said. God's Word was that they would die if they ate from the tree in the middle of the Garden. But Satan said that they "will *not* certainly die!"

- Satan questioned God's motives. According to the serpent, God did not want Adam and Eve to become like Him. Satan implied, "Maybe God is selfish or too proud to want anyone else to be like Him."

- He gave Eve only part of the truth about the forbidden tree. Yes, the fruit would open Eve's eyes. But Satan understood that to know good and evil isn't quite the desirable thing that she thought it was!

We will look at each one of these actions by Satan in the pages that follow. The Bible tells us that what he does to destroy Adam and Eve he will do to destroy us. Satan is crafty. He is a liar. He arrogantly challenges what God says. And he does it all through deception and trickery.

What can we do to protect ourselves from this evil enemy? There is only one hope. We must turn to the Creator of the universe, the one who rules everything. God can and will keep us safe from Satan's evil plots. Without His protection, we are all helpless against Satan's attacks.

Once we see Satan for who he is and how he operates, it changes our whole outlook on life. We gain insight into the evil in this world. And we learn to trust God Almighty to rescue us from these forces of wickedness.

2 What are demons? Where do demons come from?

If you do an Internet search for the word *demon*, a whole variety of results appears. There is a Demon Internet broadband service, a Demon British metal band, Demon protective gear for mountain biking and snowboarding, and Demon fuel systems for ultra-speedy automobiles. And that's just the first few online hits!

Entertainment media also exploit the word *demon* in scary supernatural stories with subjects that span from vampires to zombies. Okay, so what exactly are demons? What started all of this?

Thankfully, the Bible teaches us about demons. Like angels, demons are spirit-beings. That means they do not have physical bodies. But they are real persons. They think, reason, and have the will to make good and evil choices. In many biblical scenes, demons speak with cunning or hostility, indicating their intelligence. They also willfully torment, deceive, harass, and attack humans. They are real!

The apostle Peter tells us about demons: "God did not spare angels when they sinned, but sent them to hell, putting them in chains of darkness to be held for judgment" (2 Peter 2:4).

The passage teaches us that these demons were, in fact, angels who chose to rebel against God long ago, along with Satan. It may be that the book of Revelation describes the angelic rebellion from the distant past:

> Then war broke out in heaven. Michael and his angels fought against the dragon, and the dragon and his angels fought back. But he was not strong enough, and they lost their place in heaven. The great dragon was hurled down—that ancient serpent called the devil, or Satan, who leads the whole world astray. He was hurled to the earth, and his angels with him.
>
> Revelation 12:7–9

The apostle John describes a spectacular battle in the heavens, something we have no way to know about unless God reveals it to us. Michael, described as a prince of angels, or archangel, leads God's angels against Satan, the "great dragon," and his angels. John says that these rebelling angels "lost their place in heaven," and were "hurled down to the earth." So now, rather than serve God as pure angels, demons are corrupted by their sin. They are evil.

These demons are present on earth to interfere in human affairs in order to work out their evil ways. Jesus calls Satan the "prince of this world" (John 12:31). The apostle Paul says that the devil is "the god of this age" (2 Corinthians 4:4) and the "ruler of the kingdom of the air, the spirit who is now at work in those who are disobedient" (Ephesians 2:2).

The Bible uses several terms to describe demons. They are called spirits, evil spirits, and impure spirits (Matthew 8:16; Acts 19:13; Matthew 10:1). Paul also describes the demons as rulers, authorities, "powers of this dark world," and "spiritual forces of evil in the heavenly realms" (Ephesians 6:12). He says that they are "deceiving spirits" (1 Timothy 4:1).

What do demons look like? Since they are spirit-beings, they are invisible to us unless they choose to make themselves seen. In the Bible, though, demons are depicted in several ways. In the book of Revelation, they appear like locusts with the power of scorpions:

When [the angel] opened the Abyss, smoke rose from it like the smoke from a gigantic furnace. The sun and sky were darkened by the smoke from the Abyss. And out of the smoke locusts came down on the earth and were given power like that of scorpions of the earth.

Revelation 9:2–3

When they are unleashed, the demon-locusts make life miserable for those on the earth:

They were not allowed to kill [the people] but only to torture them for five months. And the agony they suffered was like that of the sting of a scorpion when it strikes. During those days people will seek death but will not find it; they will long to die, but death will elude them.

Revelation 9:5–6

Later in the book of Revelation, demons appear like frogs:

Then I saw three impure spirits that looked like frogs; they came out of the mouth of the dragon, out of the mouth of the beast and out of the mouth of the false prophet. They are demonic spirits that perform signs.

Revelation 16:13–14

Demons seem to be horrible creatures who can appear in many forms. They are a real enemy to be reckoned with. We must take their threat seriously.

3 What does Satan look like?

Popular images of Satan range from cute to sexy to hideous. Sometimes he is dressed all in red, with a tail, horns, pitchfork, and a mischievous smile on his face. Or Satan appears as a goat-man with red eyes and bulging muscles. Dressing like Satan for Halloween is a kid favorite. Our efforts to picture him seem to tap the extremes of human imagination.

So is there any truth to any of these images? Just what does Satan look like?

People have been trying to picture Satan for centuries. There is little agreement at the end of all of our efforts. And all of these visual portrayals of Satan through history and in popular culture point to the fact that none of us really knows what he looks like.

It is disappointing, but Satan doesn't look like any of our pictures of him, because he does not look like anything at all. Satan is a spirit-being. We cannot see him at all with our human eyes. Like God and angels, Satan exists in a spirit-reality that is outside of human ability to perceive with our senses. If they choose to, spirit-beings have the ability to appear to us in ways that we can see and hear. But in their normal form of existence, they are invisible.

The Bible does use many word pictures to describe Satan, however. In Genesis, he is portrayed as a crafty serpent that can talk: "Now the serpent was more crafty than any of the wild animals the Lord God had made" (Genesis 3:1).

The serpent image expands in several biblical passages that describe Satan as a dragon. An example is in the book of Revelation:

> And I saw an angel coming down out of heaven, having the key
> to the Abyss and holding in his hand a great chain. He seized the

dragon, that ancient serpent, who is the devil, or Satan, and bound him for a thousand years.

Revelation 20:1–2

The apostle Peter uses another vivid image for Satan: "Be alert and of sober mind. Your enemy the devil prowls around like a roaring lion looking for someone to devour" (1 Peter 5:8). Satan as a dragon or lion stirs emotions within us of a fearful creature with great power, one who preys on human beings. As such, he terrifies many people all over the world. Satan's tactics are not limited to raw power and intimidation, however. He also has a much more subtle image that appeals to us if we aren't watching for it and drop our guard. The apostle Paul warns us of his craftiness. Just as the message of the false teachers can seem appealing, Paul tells us that their master, Satan, disguises himself to deceive us:

> For such people are false apostles, deceitful workers, masquerading as apostles of Christ. And no wonder, for Satan himself masquerades as an angel of light. It is not surprising, then, if his servants also masquerade as servants of righteousness. Their end will be what their actions deserve.

2 Corinthians 11:13–15

Paul's words still hold true today. One particular satanic website makes the claim that Satan appears to those who worship him in a long white robe, with flowing blond hair.[1]

Even with all of his disguises, we still may never really know what Satan looks like. But must we know? The Bible points us to what is important here. It is not that we see Satan sufficiently to draw a picture of him. We need to recognize Satan when he attacks so that we can resist his efforts. When Peter describes Satan as a roaring lion, he warns us to "be alert and of sober mind." If we are on the alert, we will not sleepily drop our guard because we cannot see Satan with our eyes. If we are sober-minded, we will not be taken in by all of the foolish, innocent-looking ways that

Satan is pictured in our world. If we see Satan's assaults coming our way, we may be better prepared to resist him.

4 How does Satan act against humans?

All through history humans have fallen prey to Satan's attacks. Beginning with Eve in the Garden of Eden, Satan has used many methods to lure humans into sin. What are some of his tactics that he uses against us? The Bible describes several of Satan's actions.

Influences

Overall, we can see that Satan influences the decisions that we make. He used subtle persuasion against Eve in the Garden, first questioning what God had told her to do, then challenging God's command, and finally misrepresenting God's reasons for His command:

> "You will not certainly die," the serpent said to the woman. "For God knows that when you eat from [the tree] your eyes will be opened, and you will be like God, knowing good and evil."
>
> Genesis 3:4–5

Satan was also able to influence Peter's thinking when Jesus told the apostles that He was going to die when He reached Jerusalem:

> Peter took [Jesus] aside and began to rebuke him. "Never, Lord!" he said. "This shall never happen to you!" Jesus turned and said to Peter, "Get behind me, Satan! You are a stumbling block to me;

you do not have in mind the concerns of God, but merely human concerns."

Matthew 16:22–23

No doubt Peter thought that it was his idea to keep Jesus from dying. But Satan played a role inside Peter's head, planting the thought there, and Jesus recognized it.

Blinds

Satan is able to blind us. He makes it next to impossible for us to see the truth when we are exposed to it. What looks plainly obvious to most people remains a mystery to those whom Satan blinds. The apostle Paul describes this action of Satan against non-Christians, blinding them from seeing and understanding the gospel of Jesus Christ:

> And even if our gospel is veiled, it is veiled to those who are perishing. The god of this age [Satan] has blinded the minds of unbelievers, so that they cannot see the light of the gospel that displays the glory of Christ, who is the image of God.

2 Corinthians 4:3–4

Snares/Traps

Another way that Satan acts against us is by catching us in one of his traps. He sets a snare for us, just like a hunter with his prey. And the person does not see the danger until it is too late. Once captured, the helpless victim comes under the power of Satan. This is why, for example, Paul urges Christians to be patient with people who disagree with them about Christ. Why? He lets us see what is really going on:

> Opponents must be gently instructed, in the hope that God will grant them repentance leading them to a knowledge of the truth,

and that they will come to their senses and escape from the trap of the devil, who has taken them captive to do his will.

2 Timothy 2:25–26

Controls/Oppresses

Another term that the Bible uses to describe Satan's actions against us is the word *oppress*. The Greek word literally means to "overpower."[1] Satan gains a foothold in people to the point that it leads to real sickness and handicaps. One of the big things that Jesus did for people when He walked on the earth was to free them from Satan's oppression. In one of his messages, Peter makes it clear what Jesus did, and how He did it:

God anointed Jesus of Nazareth with the Holy Spirit and power, and . . . he went around doing good and healing all who were under the power of the devil, because God was with him.

Acts 10:38

The story of Jesus in the four gospels describes several cases of people under the control of Satan. Jesus extended His kindness to these people by delivering them from Satan's hand.

Possesses

The most serious term used for Satan's actions against us is when Satan *possesses* someone. Literally, someone who is demon possessed is "demonized."[2] In these cases, Satan controls or oppresses the person to the point where their will is under Satan's power. They do things at times that are personally destructive, but they cannot help it. Satan controls their will. The gospel writer Mark describes such a scene:

When Jesus got out of the boat, a man with an impure spirit came from the tombs to meet him. This man lived in the tombs, and no one could bind him anymore, not even with a chain. For he had

20

often been chained hand and foot, but he tore the chains apart and broke the irons on his feet. No one was strong enough to subdue him. Night and day among the tombs and in the hills he would cry out and cut himself with stones.

Mark 5:2–5

Later in the chapter (vv. 16, 18), Mark uses the term "demon-possessed man" two times to describe him. Notice that the man had super-human power that broke iron chains. He also purposely harmed his own body, not because he chose to, but because Satan controlled him.

What does all of this teach us about Satan? Most important, it shows us that Satan is intelligent, crafty, cunning, and persuasive. He uses different ways to gain a foothold in our lives, and he is relentless. We need to guard ourselves against his attacks.

5 How much can we really know about Satan and demons?

If we want to know about Satan and demons, there are plenty of people who will tell us all about them. Millions of websites, articles, books, films, and stories declare to us who Satan is, what he looks like, how he thinks and acts, and just about everything else that any of us would want to know. And this information comes from just about every continent, civilization, and time in history that we might wish to investigate. Yes, we have Satan and the demons pretty much figured out! Or do we?

When we push a little against all of these testimonials and "honest-to-God, true stories" about Satan and the demons, many of them give ground—sometimes a lot of ground! There is no shortage of folklore, myths, fables, fantasies, and fiction available to us about these evil creatures. Storytellers' creativity and imagination seem to know no boundaries! So we must use a good dose of caution and discernment to evaluate these stories. How do we separate the fiction from fact? How much do we really know about Satan and demons?

The Bible gives us plenty of input about Satan and demons. We can trust it to tell us the truth about them. But even biblical input is vague or incomplete at times. Even though Satan and demons are mentioned quite a bit in the Scriptures, there are very few texts that address them as the main subjects. So to get to the facts that we can trust, we must combine careful study of God's Word with credible testimonies and experiences reported from reliable people.

But let's back up for a moment. Why is there so little direct, thorough teaching about Satan and demons in the Bible? Is it because they are really not that important? Not necessarily! On the one hand, we learn from the Bible that demons are powerful, evil, and out to destroy us. They should not be taken lightly. But on the other hand, the Bible focuses much more on the things of God, humanity, and how we can enjoy a meaningful relationship with God through Jesus Christ. So perhaps we should conclude that Satan and the demons should never be ignored, but we also should not become preoccupied with them. The majority of our attention should be given to God and knowing Him.

So what do we learn from the Bible about Satan and demons? There are many passages to explore. The apostle Paul gets us started:

> Put on the full armor of God, so that you can take your stand against the devil's schemes. For our struggle is not against flesh and blood, but against the rulers, against the authorities, against the powers of this dark world and against the spiritual forces of evil in the heavenly realms.
>
> Ephesians 6:11–12

These verses tell us that demons are not flesh and blood. They do not have physical bodies like we do. They are "spiritual forces of evil," spirit-beings that live "in the heavenly realms." They live in another dimension of reality—a spiritual world—that is different from our material world. In this life, we do not have access to this heavenly realm. But demons must have access to our world or we would not be warned against them. And they are evil, hoping to use their power to bring pain and misery into our lives.

Ephesians 6:11 also informs us that Satan is crafty. He schemes against us, which implies that he is an intelligent and willful being who knows how to use his smarts against us.

The apostle Peter also adds to our knowledge of demons. He wrote, "God did not spare angels when they sinned, but sent them to hell, putting them in chains of darkness to be held for judgment" (2 Peter 2:4).

We gain many truths about demons from this passage. First, demons were angels who sinned. They were not created evil but chose to rebel against God. Second, at least some of these angels, when they sinned, were immediately cast into hell. It is a terrible place of darkness, and these fallen angels are in chains. Third, these demons are doomed. They are being "held for judgment."

Peter also said, "Be alert and of sober mind. Your enemy the devil prowls around like a roaring lion looking for someone to devour" (1 Peter 5:8).

From this passage, we learn that Satan is powerful, like a lion. Just as we would fear a lion on the loose in our presence, we should fear Satan's power and what he is able to do to us if we are not protected. And don't miss it; Satan wants to use that power against us, "looking for someone to devour." Later, we will look into some of the tactics that the devil uses against us in his efforts to harm us.

Of course, there is much more that the Bible reveals about Satan and demons. These verses we have studied are just a start, assuring us that we can know quite a bit about these evil beings. We must use what we know for sure about demons from the Bible to decide if the stories we hear are true or false. And when we face some claimed demonic experience that the Bible does not confirm, we must use great care and wisdom to evaluate it.

6 Why should I believe what the Bible says about Satan?

A wide variety of people claim to know about Satan and demons. Some say that they know Satan because they follow Satan as their master. Others say that they are dedicated to destroying him. There are even some who want to prove Satan's existence using the tools of modern science. And there are many people claiming that Satan is a figment of human imagination, coming from troubled people. There are so many sensationalized claims about Satan that it is almost impossible to discern real from fake.

There is also what the Bible says about these demonic powers.

With all of these "authorities" out there on Satan and demons, why should we listen to the Bible? What makes the Bible so special?

The Bible is a remarkable book. It is very old, dating back nearly 3,500 years. The Bible has been translated into hundreds of languages. It is the highest-selling book of all time by a wide margin.

The English translation of the Bible has shaped Western civilization and language all through its history. Dozens of expressions used in modern English come from the Bible. Examples include "a drop in the bucket," which dates back 2,700 years: "Surely the nations are like a drop in a bucket; they are regarded as dust on the scales" (Isaiah 40:15).

To make a narrow escape "by the skin of your teeth" comes from an expression first used centuries before Jesus Christ: "I am nothing but skin and bones; I have escaped only by the skin of my teeth" (Job 19:20).

Despite the Bible's major role in shaping our civilization, it is one of the world's least understood books. It seems as though everyone has an opinion about the Bible, but few have actually read it. When we dive into its pages, we discover that the Bible claims to be the Word of God. God has chosen to reveal himself to us in the words of the Bible. He teaches us about the world around us and who we are as human beings, His creatures. We learn what it means to come to know God. We understand how we can relate to God personally.

And we learn quite a lot about Satan and the demons in the pages of the Bible.

But is the Bible a reliable source of truth about Satan or anything else? We need to realize that the Bible's teachings have been tested for centuries and found to be true. Archaeological research repeatedly confirms the historical details recorded in the Bible.

Because God speaks through the pages of Scripture, many miraculous predictions are recorded as well. One of the most remarkable prophecies of the Bible is in the book of Isaiah. The prophet records God's words for a Persian king, Cyrus. Isaiah says that God is the one

> who says of Cyrus, "He is my shepherd
> and will accomplish all that I please;
> he will say of Jerusalem, 'Let it be rebuilt,'
> and of the temple, 'Let its foundations be laid.'"
> Isaiah 44:28

When we put in the dates for this statement, the prophecy is amazing. Isaiah lived 150 years before Cyrus. Yet God calls out Cyrus by name through Isaiah and declares that Cyrus will see to it that the temple in Jerusalem will be rebuilt. Sure enough, Cyrus commanded that the Jews return to Jerusalem in 538 BC to rebuild the temple:

In the first year of Cyrus king of Persia, in order to fulfill the word of the Lord spoken by Jeremiah, the Lord moved the heart of Cyrus

25

king of Persia to make a proclamation throughout his realm and also to put it in writing: "This is what Cyrus king of Persia says: 'The Lord, the God of heaven, has given me all the kingdoms of the earth and he has appointed me to build a temple for him at Jerusalem in Judah.'"

Ezra 1:1–2

What the Bible says about Satan and demons is reported in sober, informative language. Other sources reveal their superstition, fear, and unhealthy fascination with Satan, causing their claims about Satan to be full of errors, exaggeration, and speculation. The Bible's teaching about demonic powers stands in stark contrast to all of that. It has the ring of truth, and history backs its claims about Satan.

Perhaps the best thing you can do is to read what the Bible has to say about Satan and demons. Judge for yourself if the words of Scripture are true. And test God in this. Ask God to confirm for you the truthfulness of the Bible in a way that you cannot mistake. Seek out the truth for yourself.

There is an odd paradox about the Bible. To mockers, the Bible remains a closed book. They have great difficulty understanding its teaching. But for seekers, the Bible unlocks many of the secrets of existence. God communicates to them. Jesus teaches that His words find two different results in people:

> The disciples came to [Jesus] and asked, "Why do you speak to the people in parables?"
>
> He replied, "Because the knowledge of the secrets of the kingdom of heaven has been given to you, but not to them. Whoever has will be given more, and they will have an abundance. Whoever does not have, even what they have will be taken from them. This is why I speak to them in parables: 'Though seeing, they do not see; though hearing, they do not hear or understand.'"
>
> Matthew 13:10–13

The disciples of Jesus were seekers, so Jesus' teaching was profitable for them. Those who opposed Jesus did not understand His teaching. They did not want to know the truth, so it was kept from them.

Those who read with an open, seeking heart what the Scriptures have to say about Satan can trust the Scriptures to tell them the truth. Test the Bible for yourself. You will not be disappointed.

7 What is demon possession?

Some of the scariest movies in the last fifty years depict demon possession. A few of us remember *The Omen* and *Rosemary's Baby*. But *The Exorcist* was tops. Released in 1973, *The Exorcist* tells the fictional tale of a child possessed by a demon manifesting several scary, gross behaviors. Movie houses reported people getting sick during the movie, running out of theaters. But *The Exorcist* was wildly popular, taking the world by storm. It grossed over $400 million worldwide, more than any horror movie before. It was voted the scariest movie of all time by several entertainment publications.[1]

What is demon possession? Literally, it means to be "demonized."[2] A person comes under such complete demonic influence that the person cannot control their actions or decisions. The demon can force its host to do whatever it wants, sometimes with superhuman power.

The Bible records several instances of demon possession. For example, the gospel writer Mark reports the following incident:

[Jesus and the apostles] went across the lake to the region of the Gerasenes. When Jesus got out of the boat, a man with an impure spirit came from the tombs to meet him. This man lived in the tombs, and no one could bind him anymore, not even with a chain. For he had often been chained hand and foot, but he tore the chains apart and broke the irons on his feet. No one was strong enough to subdue him. Night and day among the tombs and in the hills he would cry out and cut himself with stones.

Mark 5:1–5

This poor man was demonized to the point where he was uncontrollable. Even iron chains could not subdue him. And the demon was tormenting him to the point where he harmed himself. Evidently this man could not control himself. The demon possessed him.

Demon possession is illustrated again in Mark's gospel, four chapters later:

When the spirit saw Jesus, it immediately threw the boy into a convulsion. He fell to the ground and rolled around, foaming at the mouth.

Jesus asked the boy's father, "How long has he been like this?"

"From childhood," he answered. "It has often thrown him into fire or water to kill him. But if you can do anything, take pity on us and help us."

Mark 9:20–22

Similar to the previous story, under the spirit's power, the boy loses control of his body. And the evil spirit seeks to kill the boy, either through burning or drowning him. We don't know how old this boy is when Jesus meets him, but he has been under the demon's power since childhood.

Two more things stand out in this incident. First, the demon inside the child immediately reacts when Jesus comes into view. Evidently, the spirit does not like the powerful Lord Jesus Christ coming so close. And second, it does not seem possible that the boy has done something to invite demonic attack, since he was just a young child when it started. Other factors might have contributed to his demonization, but Scripture does not tell us what those reasons were.

What causes demon possession? A clear answer escapes us. No cause is ever indicated directly in the Bible. Jesus gives us some help, but His words remain shrouded in enough mystery to generate more questions about the cause of demon possession than He answers. One passage in particular illustrates the difficulty of understanding how demon possession happens. Jesus teaches that

> when an impure spirit comes out of a person, it goes through arid places seeking rest and does not find it. Then it says, "I will return to the house I left." When it arrives, it finds the house swept clean and put in order. Then it goes and takes seven other spirits more wicked than itself, and they go in and live there. And the final condition of that person is worse than the first.
>
> Luke 11:24–26

We simply do not know exactly what Jesus means by the impure spirit returning to the house that he left, finding that house "swept clean and put in order." Jesus seems to say that someone whose life is in order still can be vulnerable to demonization, especially if they have had a history of demon influence.

Two common links surface, though, as causes for demons gaining control over someone. The first is when someone dabbles in occult activity. Seemingly harmless entertainment or curiosity may open a door to demon influence. A popular example today is the practice of divination (trying to know the future) through a Ouija board or through holding a séance. Few participants realize the demonic power lurking behind such "harmless" games.

A second link to demonic activity is coming under the control of ongoing sin in one's life. Jesus himself teaches that sin brings us under its control: "Very truly I tell you, everyone who sins is a slave to sin" (John 8:34).

Sin has the power to control us. It can lead to habits and addictions that overwhelm our ability to say no to them. It appears possible that demons can exploit sin's control by asserting their own presence in our lives. These are deep and ominous warnings for us to resist temptation and to stay clear of demonic influence in all of its forms.

8 What is exorcism?

Demonization is a terrible thing. Someone who is demonized deserves our compassion. Dark powers have such a hold on the person that they no longer have the ability to control themselves. Is there any hope for such misery and bondage? The Bible says yes. Demons can be ousted from their control over someone. The word most associated with this action is *exorcism*.

What is exorcism? The Greek word for *exorcise* means to "extract an oath"[1] and is associated with expelling one or more demons from a human host. An exorcist is someone who possesses the power and authority to cast out demons.

Demon exorcisms have been practiced for centuries in many world religions, including Christianity.[2] Within Christian traditions, many rituals and beliefs are practiced.[3]

The Bible contains many instances of demon exorcism. As we would expect, the Lord Jesus Christ cast out many demons from afflicted people during His years on earth. The gospel writer Matthew tells us that Jesus also gave His followers the ability to exorcise demons: "Jesus called his twelve disciples to him and gave them authority to drive out impure spirits and to heal every disease and sickness" (Matthew 10:1).

When Jesus cast out demons, the Bible records that it seemed almost effortless for Him. When He spoke, the demons left immediately. For His followers, however, there appeared to be more of a challenge at times. After Jesus revealed His glory to Peter, James, and John on a mountain, He came back to find His disciples wrestling with a case of demon possession. Mark records the scene:

> A man in the crowd answered, "Teacher, I brought you my son, who is possessed by a spirit that has robbed him of speech. Whenever it seizes him, it throws him to the ground. He foams at the mouth, gnashes his teeth and becomes rigid. I asked your disciples to drive out the spirit, but they could not."

Mark 9:17–18

After Jesus delivers the boy from the demon and the crowds have gone, His disciples ask Jesus about it: "'Why couldn't we drive it out?' He replied, 'This kind can come out only by prayer'" (Mark 9:28–29).

Jesus teaches the disciples that some demonic possessions are more severe than others. It may be that the disciples forgot that their ability to exorcise demons came from God, through prayer. It was not some power they had over demons. Jesus delegated God's power to them over the demons.

We learn more about demon exorcism from an incident in Matthew's gospel:

> Leaving that place, Jesus withdrew to the region of Tyre and Sidon. A Canaanite woman from that vicinity came to him, crying out, "Lord, Son of David, have mercy on me! My daughter is demon-possessed and suffering terribly."
>
> Jesus did not answer a word. So his disciples came to him and urged him, "Send her away, for she keeps crying out after us."
>
> He answered, "I was sent only to the lost sheep of Israel."
>
> The woman came and knelt before him. "Lord, help me!" she said.
>
> He replied, "It is not right to take the children's bread and toss it to the dogs."
>
> "Yes it is, Lord," she said. "Even the dogs eat the crumbs that fall from their master's table."

Then Jesus said to her, "Woman, you have great faith! Your request is granted." And her daughter was healed at that moment.

Matthew 15:21–28

Look at several things here. First, the demonized girl does not ask Jesus to be delivered; her mother does. There is never a case in the Bible where the demon-possessed person is able to ask for deliverance from the demon. Someone else must seek the exorcism.

Even more important, Jesus responds to the woman's persistent faith. She will not be dismissed, even when Jesus looks disinterested in her plight. Exorcism is linked to a relentless, enduring trust in Jesus Christ to heal the person. There does not seem to be any pre-scribed ritual or formula for demons to be expelled. Jesus casts out demons in a variety of ways in the gospels. But utter dependence on Christ is the common factor in every case.

Demons are powerful and dangerous. We cannot face them on our own, thinking that we possess the power to cast out demons. We must act with full trust in God to display His power.

Should we attempt to exorcise demons? On the one hand, Jesus has given His followers the authority to cast out demons. But on the other hand, exorcism is a serious action against dangerous foes. We should exercise caution when taking on Satan and evil spirits. Many church traditions urge their people to involve church leaders, such as pastors or elders, in any attempt to engage demons.

9 Is demon possession the same thing as mental illness?

The Bible records several scenes where people are sick or act in ways that are disturbing. In many of the biblical accounts, the authors attribute human sickness to demonic causes. For example, the gospel writer Mark records Jesus confronting a man with an unclean spirit:

> This man lived in the tombs, and no one could bind him anymore, not even with a chain. For he had often been chained hand and foot, but he tore the chains apart and broke the irons on his feet. No one was strong enough to subdue him. Night and day among the tombs and in the hills he would cry out and cut himself with stones.
>
> Mark 5:3–5

The demonized man is troubled mentally, with physical symptoms, too. However, Mark reports a major change after Jesus exorcizes the demons: "When [the people] came to Jesus, they saw the man who had been possessed by the legion of demons, sitting there, dressed and in his right mind; and they were afraid" (Mark 5:15).

In another scene from Mark's gospel, a sick boy displays several physical and psychological maladies:

> A man in the crowd answered, "Teacher, I brought you my son, who is possessed by a spirit that has robbed him of speech. Whenever it seizes him, it throws him to the ground. He foams at the mouth, gnashes his teeth and becomes rigid. . . . It has often thrown him into fire or water to kill him."
>
> Mark 9:17–18, 22

The demon keeps the child from speaking. The boy also convulses under the spirit's control. And the demon makes him try to harm himself. Clearly, both physical and emotional manifestations come from the spirit's attacks.

How should we understand the implications of the Bible's teaching about demon possession and mental illness today? Through the study of medicine and psychology, we have learned a lot in the last two centuries about how the mind works. Conditions such as depression, psychosis, and dissociative identity disorder were not understood in Bible times. For those of us who recognize the Bible

33

as true in all that it teaches, how do we understand Satan's role in emotional sickness?

Much of modern psychiatry disputes the influence of demons.[1] Physical or psychological causes are cited for symptoms that were associated with demonism in the past. However, Christian psychologists generally recognize the influence of spiritual forces in physical and emotional illness. For example, the Christian Medical Fellowship published an article titled "Demon Possession and Mental Illness" in 1997.[2] The author identifies several diagnostic paths to be explored—spiritual, social, psychological, and physical—when people display physical or psychological disorders. Are these Christian psychologists on the right road to understanding mental illness, or is the mainstream position held by most doctors today the correct stance? There are a few ideas to consider.

First, the Bible attributes mental disorders to demonic causes. But the Bible also appears to distinguish physical and mental illness from demonic activity. For example, Mark summarizes the healing work of Jesus in one village:

> That evening after sunset the people brought to Jesus all the sick and demon-possessed. The whole town gathered at the door, and Jesus healed many who had various diseases. He also drove out many demons, but he would not let the demons speak because they knew who he was.
>
> Mark 1:32–34

Mark divides the people coming to Jesus into two groups—the sick and the demon possessed. He also separates those with various diseases from those who were demonized. The Bible recognizes a difference between demon activity and illness.

Furthermore, we need to admit that what we know through science about the human mind is still growing rapidly. There is still much that science does not understand about the brain and the mind. Discoveries over the last few decades have advanced our grasp of the functioning of the human mind, but quite a bit remains a mystery to us.

In particular, a lively discussion persists among medical experts over basic human nature. Some naturalists claim that humans are no more than physical beings. All human thoughts, feelings, choices, and behavior are explainable through complex biochemical processes in the brain, according to the naturalist. We have no soul, spirit, or conscience.

Christian psychologists point to the Bible's teaching that humans are more than merely physical beings. For instance, note Jesus' warning about the fear of death: "Do not be afraid of those who kill the body but cannot kill the soul. Rather, be afraid of the One who can destroy both soul and body in hell" (Matthew 10:28).

Christian psychology remains open to many potential causes of mental illness—physical, emotional, social, and spiritual. Christian psychologists are challenged to consider several possible causes when treating someone suffering emotional illness.

Indeed, many terrible stories have circulated about people who are suffering emotionally being subject to exorcisms or healing through prayer, as if spiritual causes are the only possible explanation for the illness. That may be as big a mistake as limiting the causes of mental illness to simply physical explanations.

The Bible appears to leave open the door to explain physical and emotional illnesses. Demons may be involved at times, but not necessarily. Our approach to help those who suffer such sicknesses must expand to cover every possibility.

10 Can a demon possess a follower of Christ?

A practical question emerges from the last chapter. Demon possession sounds very serious. And it is! No one should treat the issue lightly. If demons are able to live inside of someone, controlling the person's body, mind, and will, it seems clear that all of us should want to avoid such a condition completely.

For those who call themselves Christians—followers of Christ—demonization is a terrifying thought. One of the most frequent questions I receive about Satan and demons from Christian college students is, "Can a follower of Christ be demon possessed?" Often it appears that the person is worried about their own situation or someone close to them. Their anxiety grows the more they consider the possibility. "Can Satan ever take control of me or someone I love? Or am I protected from demonization because I am a follower of Christ?"

At first glance, the Bible teaches that no, a Christ-follower cannot be possessed by a demon. One of the benefits of following Christ is that God the Holy Spirit himself actually lives in our bodies. The apostle Paul teaches, "Do you not know that your bodies are temples of the Holy Spirit, who is in you, whom you have received from God? You are not your own" (1 Corinthians 6:19).

If the Holy Spirit is with those of us who follow Christ, living in our bodies, then a demon cannot also live inside of us. The Holy Spirit would give the evil spirit the boot! We are protected from demonic control by God's Spirit. That's reassuring!

We need to consider a few important issues, however, that make the question a little more complicated.

First, what is a true follower of Christ? People all over the globe claim to be Christians, but what they mean by that label varies a

36

lot. Here are twelve things that aren't enough to make someone a true follower of Christ, even if they claim to be a Christian:

- I go to church.
- I try to be a good person (most of the time).
- I pray to God.
- I receive the Lord's Supper when I go to church.
- I was baptized as a kid.
- I give money to the church.
- I teach Sunday school.
- I come from a Christian family.
- I smile at the pastor when I see him.
- I don't drink, smoke, gamble, swear, or watch racy movies.
- I read the Bible.
- I bathe regularly.

A true follower of Christ is more than these things. Real Christians are followers of Christ. They trust Jesus to forgive their sins through His death on the cross. Christ means everything to them. Listen to the apostle Peter: "All the prophets testify about [Jesus] that everyone who believes in him receives forgiveness of sins through his name" (Acts 10:43).

If someone is not a true follower of Christ, they may be able to be demon possessed.

A second issue affects the answer we give to the question, "Can a true follower of Christ be demon possessed?" Is it possible for a true Christ-follower to stop being one? Can a real Christian quit being a Christian?

Christian teachers do not all agree on what the Bible says about those who stop following Christ. It is a big issue, too complicated for us to discuss in sufficient detail in this study. But there is a practical side to the issue. If someone trusts Christ to take away their sins and continues to follow after Christ sincerely, virtually all Bible-believing Christians agree that the person is secure in their faith in Christ. They cannot just stop being a follower of Christ by accident. No evil spirit can possess them.

The problem comes when someone claims to be a follower of Christ, but then turns their back on Christ and either renounces their faith in Jesus or becomes enslaved to sin willingly and defiantly. We could argue with each other endlessly whether this person ever was a true Christ-follower. But we would agree that the person is not a follower of Christ now, by their own admission. They are vulnerable to demon attack, and maybe even demon possession.

Can a true follower of Christ be demon possessed? A third issue we must address compares demon *oppression* to demon *possession*. Demon oppression means that someone is experiencing demonic attacks. The person may suffer physically, emotionally, or spiritually. But they manage to remain in control of their will. They still can make choices on their own. A demon-possessed person, however, loses control of their will. The evil spirit makes them do things they do not choose to do. They are helplessly under the demon's control.

Therefore, technically, a true follower of Christ cannot be possessed by a demon. But Christ-followers are still subject to demon oppression if they choose to dabble in sin or activities that invite demon activity. This should be a warning to those who follow Christ. Do not think that you are protected from the dark powers no matter what. Demons can make your life miserable if you play around with demonic, occult activities or you choose to flirt with sin. Why would you want to play around with evil? If you sincerely love Christ and desire to follow Him, you will choose to stay far away from all evil.

The Bible teaches us that those who follow Christ can be reassured of His care and protection against demonic possession as they love Christ and continue to follow Him wholeheartedly: "The one who is in you [the Holy Spirit] is greater than the one who is in the world [Satan and the demons]" (1 John 4:4).

Those who follow Christ, seeking to please Him with their lives, need not fear demon possession. Jesus Christ will look out for His own people.

11 What does it mean to be a follower of Jesus Christ?

Satan and the demons are formidable enemies. We have seen from the Bible that only those who are followers of Jesus Christ have any hope of protection from these dark powers. But what does it mean to be a follower of Jesus Christ?

The Bible is crystal clear. Followers of Christ identify with Him. They know who Jesus claims to be, and they put their trust in His claims, believing that they are true. Two of Christ's claims are most important, straight from the Bible.

First, Jesus Christ claims to be God himself, the second person in the Trinity, the eternal Son. Many biblical texts teach that Jesus is God. One of the clearest is when Jesus declared himself to be God. Listen to the exchange between Jesus and the Jews who opposed Him:

"Your father Abraham rejoiced at the thought of seeing my day; he saw it and was glad."

"You are not yet fifty years old," [the Jews] said to him, "and you have seen Abraham!"

"Very truly I tell you," Jesus answered, "before Abraham was born, I am!" At this, they picked up stones to stone him, but Jesus hid himself, slipping away from the temple grounds.

John 8:56–59

Jesus lived 2,000 years after Abraham, the great founder of the Hebrew people. However, not only did Jesus claim to be older than Abraham, He said that Abraham looked forward to Jesus' time. And the real blockbuster was when Jesus said, *"I am!"* Centuries earlier, God revealed to Moses what His name is: "God said to Moses, 'I am who I am. This is what you are to say to the Israelites: "I am has sent me to you"'" (Exodus 3:14).

There was no mistaking it! When Jesus said, "before Abraham was born, I am," He was claiming to be the same God who appeared to Moses in Exodus. That is why the Jews were ready to kill Jesus right then and there. They knew that Jesus was claiming to be God, to them a crime worthy of death.

Jesus is not merely a good teacher, a prophet, or a holy man. Jesus is God! In fact, if He is not God, then He isn't good at all. He is either a liar or just plain crazy to claim that He is God. But if Jesus Christ truly is the Lord God Almighty, the demons dread His power. We can find protection from Satan with Jesus.

Jesus also claimed in the Bible that He would die as a sacrifice for sin—all sin that all humans have ever committed and ever will commit in the future. John the Baptist proclaimed Jesus as the sacrifice for human sin: "The next day John saw Jesus coming toward him and said, 'Look, the Lamb of God, who takes away the sin of the world!'" (John 1:29).

Jesus himself warned those who opposed Him, "I told you that you would die in your sins; if you do not believe that I am he, you will indeed die in your sins" (John 8:24).

You see, all of us have sinned—both large and small sins—and that sin separates us from God and gains control over us. We cannot escape the power of sin; we are helpless. Jesus stated it bluntly: "Very truly I tell you, everyone who sins is a slave to sin" (John 8:34).

But Jesus came to take our place. He died for our sin so that we can be pardoned and be free from its power. The apostle Paul explains our problem and the solution in two simple verses: "For all have sinned and fall short of the glory of God" (Romans 3:23) and "For the wages of sin is death, but the gift of God is eternal life in Christ Jesus our Lord" (Romans 6:23).

All of us are sinners. We cannot free ourselves from sin's grip. We earn death by sinning; it is our wages. At the last judgment, we will be found guilty and forever separated from God. But God's gift of eternal life comes to us through Jesus because He loves us. Jesus claims, in the most famous Bible verse of all, that God's love motivated Him to send Jesus Christ: "For God so loved the world that he gave his one and only Son, that whoever believes in him shall not perish but have eternal life" (John 3:16).

Paul echoes these words:

> You see, at just the right time, when we were still powerless, Christ died for the ungodly. Very rarely will anyone die for a righteous person, though for a good person someone might possibly dare to die. But God demonstrates his own love for us in this: While we were still sinners, Christ died for us.
>
> Romans 5:6–8

Jesus Christ is God. He died to free us from sin and to forgive our sins so that we can know God and be free! Followers of Jesus depend on these claims. They stake their present and future lives on Jesus. They believe, "If Jesus is not God, and if Jesus does not forgive my sin, then I have no hope of reaching God."

When we put our trust in Jesus, He becomes the one we love more than anyone. He has saved us from sin, bondage, and death. He gives us peace with God. And we will live forever with Him. Paul's own life illustrates this love and devotion to Christ:

> But whatever were gains to me I now consider loss for the sake of Christ. What is more, I consider everything a loss because of the surpassing worth of knowing Christ Jesus my Lord, for whose sake I have lost all things. I consider them garbage, that I may gain Christ.
>
> Philippians 3:7–8

In their hearts, followers of Jesus feel the same way. They willingly forsake everything else to be with Christ. And one of the benefits of following Christ has to do with Satan. If we want to come under God's protection from Satan and his demons, we must become followers of Christ.

12 How can I become a follower of Jesus?

All over the world, people identify themselves as Christians. The president of the United States, star athletes, pop music artists, and business tycoons all gain attention by declaring to be Christians. Add to that millions of people around the world who attend church meetings regularly in the name of Jesus Christ.

Over one billion people on planet earth embrace the label "Christian." What they think it means to be a Christian, though, varies a lot. Some claim that church membership is essential. Many believe that participating in church rituals like the Lord's Supper is required. Still others think that being a Christian means that they must live according to a specific moral code of right and wrong, like the Ten Commandments. It seems like being a Christian is whatever people make it out to be. Is there any way to know what is true?

Our study assumes that the final authority for the Christian faith comes from the pages of the Bible. All human opinion is judged by what the Bible teaches.

Even though the word *Christian* is used in the Bible, the phrase that best describes what it means to be a Christian according to the Bible is *follower of Christ*. The Scriptures often use the word *disciple* to describe a Christian. For instance, when Jesus sends the apostles out with His message, notice how He says it:

Then Jesus came to [the apostles] and said, "All authority in heaven and on earth has been given to me. Therefore go and make disciples of all nations, baptizing them in the name of the Father and of the Son and of the Holy Spirit, and teaching them to obey everything I have commanded you. And surely I am with you always, to the very end of the age."

Matthew 28:18–20

The Greek word translated "disciple" means pupil or follower.[1] A disciple of Jesus Christ follows Him. This book uses *follower of Christ* to describe a Christian.

We learned in the last chapter that a follower of Christ loves Jesus more than anything or anyone else. Christ's followers trust that Jesus is God Almighty and that Jesus' death on the cross forgives their sin, gives them peace with God, and grants them eternal life. In response, those who follow Christ will do anything Jesus wants them to do because they love Him. They are filled with gratitude over what He has done for them.

Those who follow Jesus Christ also come under God's protection against Satan and demons.

So then, how exactly do you become a follower of Jesus Christ? Quite simply, by putting your faith in Jesus. All of us have a decision to make. Will we try to reach God on our own? Or will we trust Jesus Christ the Savior to pay the penalty for our sins, saving us from eternal death, so that we may know God? If we seek safety from Satan and demons, we must trust Christ to save us from our sins.

What's important here is that we decide to trust Jesus. How we express that trust can vary. Some people speak out loud to God. They may say something like this: "Jesus, I believe you are God. I trust you alone to take away my sins and to give me peace with God." Or some might just make the commitment to trust Jesus in the quiet places of their hearts, never actually saying anything out loud.

Many Christian traditions connect the decision to trust Jesus with water baptism. By being baptized, believers are saying to God, to the world, and to themselves that they depend on Jesus to save them from their sins.

What really matters is that we choose to trust Jesus as our Savior. How we express that trust isn't nearly as important as actually *doing* it. And the Bible says that when we make the decision, wonderful things happen! It is as if our lives begin again. We are new persons. We have peace with God. And we will live forever with Jesus. Knowing Jesus Christ and being close to Him means more to us than anything.

We also receive God's protection against Satan and the dark host. We stand little chance against them on our own. But the Bible teaches that Satan and the demons tremble before God Almighty and the Lord Jesus Christ. Listen to the fear in their voices when Jesus confronts them: "'What do you want with us, Son of God?' [the demons] shouted. 'Have you come here to torture us before the appointed time [of judgment]?'" (Matthew 8:29).

Our only hope against these dark spirits is to seek the protection that Jesus Christ alone can offer. Nothing else will do. If you have not decided to trust Jesus to forgive your sins, what are you waiting for? There is nothing to lose but your bondage to sin. And there is everything to gain!

13 Can Satan read my thoughts? Can he place thoughts in my mind?

Dramatizing mind control is a popular, scary way to entertain us. Entertainment media portray weak-willed humans coming under the spell of aliens, Jedi knights, or sorcerers employing the "evil eye" to bind us to their will. For some of us, it's all good fun because the thought of mind control taps a subconscious fear we have of coming under someone else's power.

The fun diminishes, however, when we consider the possibility that Satan has access to our minds, an evil mastermind with the ability to manipulate us. Is Satan able to read my thoughts? Can he place thoughts into my mind? The Bible is not entirely clear with an answer.

One of the challenges comes in understanding the relationship between the two spheres of existence—the physical world and the spiritual domain. How much traffic travels from one sphere to the other?

On the one hand, we humans do not normally have access to the spirit-realm until we die. Some people claim access to the spirit domain in this life through occult practices or through near-death experiences. These are special claims that are out of the ordinary for most people.

We do know, however, that spirits—angels, demons, and God himself—have free access to our world. It appears they can interact in our physical domain any time they choose. The Bible never shows a barrier or roadblock that spirit-beings must overcome to act within the physical universe. They can even invade our bodies, as Satan did with Judas during the Last Supper: "As soon as Judas took the bread, Satan entered into him" (John 13:27).

The Bible also confirms that Satan and demons have access to our minds and thoughts. In the same scene at the Last Supper, Satan influenced Judas's thoughts: "The evening meal was in progress, and the devil had already prompted Judas, the son of Simon Iscariot, to betray Jesus" (John 13:2).

Satan did not physically appear that night, standing behind Judas, whispering in his ear. The verse literally says that the devil had already "put it into the heart" (ESV) of Judas the thought to betray Jesus.

A similar incident happened a thousand years before Judas lived. Satan persuaded King David to do something he should not have done. "Satan rose up against Israel and incited David to take a census of Israel" (1 Chronicles 21:1).

The verse does not spell out exactly how Satan incited David to number Israel. But a likely explanation is that Satan placed the thought in David's mind.

What the Bible teaches is confirmed for many of us through our experience. A number of people testify to thoughts coming into their heads out of nowhere, horrible thoughts to harm themselves or others. For example, while walking across a high bridge, someone senses the prompting to "Jump!" Where did that come from? The person is relatively happy and stable emotionally, so it does not seem possible that the suggestion to commit suicide came from their own mind or heart. Perhaps Satan and demons are responsible for placing such outrageous ideas into our heads.

Can Satan also read our minds? No clear biblical evidence supports the idea. Only God knows everything, not Satan or any other creature. The devil is very clever, though, and he has been a student of human nature for thousands of years. Just compare: Even when we have a close friend or family member, we can often "read their minds" accurately by observing their body language and facial expressions. We can predict accurately what they are going to do because we know them. Satan can do the same, too, because he knows us. He sees us react to situations in ways that make it pretty easy to discern what we are thinking. He knows us very well, including our weaknesses. And he can exploit those weaknesses.

Behind all of this is a bigger reality—our many vulnerabilities as humans. As much as we like to proclaim our strengths as a human race, multiple forces can influence, manipulate, or deceive us, including Satan. So many sins are conceived in our thought life. We are creatures susceptible to many forces.

A word of caution: If you are hearing voices in your head, please speak to someone about it. The voices may come from demons, or they may signal other emotional issues you need to address. Either way, seek someone's help. Even if the voices seem harmless or offer companionship, this is not something to dismiss.

We can resist Satan by watching over our minds and hearts carefully. Consider two suggestions: First, entrust your mind to the Lord Jesus Christ. Become a follower of Jesus and ask Him to guard your heart against such awful thoughts and feelings. Remember, He is the Lord of all, commanding the demons as they tremble before Him.

Second, as Christ-followers, we can also make good choices about what we allow into our heads. If we fill our minds with worldly, ungodly input, we can expect to struggle with our thought life. Rather, if we take the advice of the apostle Paul, we can avoid a lot of difficulties:

> Finally, brothers and sisters, whatever is true, whatever is noble, whatever is right, whatever is pure, whatever is lovely, whatever is admirable—if anything is excellent or praiseworthy—think about such things. Whatever you have learned or received or heard from me, or seen in me—put it into practice. And the God of peace will be with you.
>
> Philippians 4:8–9

We can experience the peace of God when we devote our thoughts to these things. Satan may still have access, but he will find that he is attacking a much stronger person, one who is prepared to resist his efforts.

14 Was Satan created by God? How did Satan become evil?

Satan is the poster boy for evil. No other person or idea captures the horror of wickedness like him. It is Satan's nature to be evil.

God, on the other hand, defines love and goodness. He is the one who does the kind and caring thing merely by being himself. It is His nature to be good.

Those who are followers of Jesus Christ believe that God created the universe and everything in it. If that is true, did the perfectly good God create Satan? The simple answer is yes, but there is more to it.

God made the world out of nothing. He gives it all meaning. Everything that exists comes from the hand of God. The creation story in Genesis portrays the formation of the human race as the crowning event:

> So God created mankind in his own image, in the image of God he created them; male and female he created them. God blessed them and said to them, "Be fruitful and increase in number; fill the earth and subdue it. Rule over the fish in the sea and the birds in the sky and over every living creature that moves on the ground."
>
> Genesis 1:27–28

We look to God as the one who made the human race in His image. He gave us jurisdiction over the world. But there is no mention of the creation of angels or Satan in Genesis. The story is limited to God's creation of the physical universe, not the spiritual realm in which angels and demons live. Their creation is not recorded in any of the historical sections of the Bible.

There are two biblical passages in the Prophets, though, that may give us some clues to Satan's creation and fall into sin. The first text comes from the prophet Isaiah. The prophet declares that Israel will "take up this taunt against the king of Babylon" (Isaiah 14:3). Part of the prophecy intrigues us:

> How you have fallen from heaven,
>   morning star, son of the dawn!
> You have been cast down to the earth,
>   you who once laid low the nations!

You said in your heart,
   "I will ascend to the heavens;
I will raise my throne
   above the stars of God;
I will sit enthroned on the mount of assembly,
   on the utmost heights of Mount Zaphon.
I will ascend above the tops of the clouds;
   I will make myself like the Most High."
But you are brought down to the realm of the dead,
   to the depths of the pit.

Isaiah 14:12–15

Interpreting the prophecy is difficult. It is hard to know exactly who is the object of the taunt. It is addressed to the king of Babylon, a human ruler. But much of the language appears to describe someone who is not a human being. How can a human "have fallen from heaven"? And the word translated "morning star" literally means "shining one."[1] It is the word from which popular culture gets the word *Lucifer* for Satan.[2] At least some interpreters have seen this taunt describing more than a human king of Babylon. It depicts Satan's sin of pride, thinking he can reach the heights of heaven and even displace God himself on His throne. However, prophecies often use exaggerated expressions to make their points, so Isaiah may be, after all, describing the king of Babylon in extreme language.

The second prophecy brings in the same interpretive difficulties. Similar to Isaiah, the prophet Ezekiel is told to take up a lament for the king of Tyre:

You were the seal of perfection,
   full of wisdom and perfect in beauty.
You were in Eden,
   the garden of God;
every precious stone adorned you:
   carnelian, chrysolite and emerald,
   topaz, onyx and jasper,
   lapis lazuli, turquoise and beryl.

Your settings and mountings were made of gold;
    on the day you were created they were prepared.
You were anointed as a guardian cherub,
    for so I ordained you.
You were on the holy mount of God;
    you walked among the fiery stones.
You were blameless in your ways
    from the day you were created
    till wickedness was found in you.
Through your widespread trade
    you were filled with violence,
    and you sinned.
So I drove you in disgrace from the mount of God,
    and I expelled you, guardian cherub,
    from among the fiery stones.
Your heart became proud
    on account of your beauty,
and you corrupted your wisdom
    because of your splendor.
So I threw you to the earth;
    I made a spectacle of you before kings.

Ezekiel 28:12–17

The "king of Tyre" is a human ruler. But the subject of the lament is described as having been created as the guardian cherub on God's holy mount. A cherub is an angelic being who in other Scripture passages is associated closely with God. Two figures of cherubim were made over the ark of the covenant in Israel's tabernacle, overshadowing the presence of God (Hebrews 9:5). So this person in Ezekiel appears to be an angelic creature who falls into sin because of his pride and vanity.

Are these two prophecies referring to Satan's fall? Biblical interpreters disagree. The question remains unresolved. We *do* know, however, that this creature was created by God along with everything else. And all of God's creation was good; the Bible emphatically repeats the point six times in the first chapter of Genesis.

Satan had fallen into sin by the time he appeared as a serpent in the Garden of Eden in Genesis. How he sinned is not explained for us clearly.

The fate of the creature who became the devil illustrates what happened to the earth and the human race, too. God created the earth good and perfect. But something terrible happened. Sin entered creation and corrupted it. The apostle Paul explains:

> The creation itself will be liberated from its bondage to decay and brought into the freedom and glory of the children of God. We know that the whole creation has been groaning as in the pains of childbirth right up to the present time.
>
> Romans 8:21–22

In particular, Adam and Eve were created good. When they sinned, they brought sin and corruption to the entire human race.

God created the person who became Satan. But God created him, and everything else, perfect and good. Sin spoiled God's creation. God's plan, however, is to renew His creation through Jesus Christ. What began perfect will again be good when all sin and evil are banished forever.

15 Is Satan responsible for every bad thing that happens, like war, famine, earthquakes, etc.?

Our world is full of disasters. We can glance at news headlines anytime to find wars, earthquakes, mass murders, famine, and every conceivable kind of heartache. In our own lives, there is usually enough tragedy to occupy us. Life contains difficulty, pain, and evil. So the question presents itself to us: Is Satan the one to blame for all of the pain and evil in the world? Does every bad thing that happens come from the hand of Satan?

We cannot answer the question with the kind of certainty that we would like. Satan's actions are not easily identified openly in the world. We lack the kind of proof needed to pin all evil and tragedy on Satan. The Bible gives us a look behind the scenes, however, to inform us of Satan's role when evil strikes.

The first two chapters of the book of Job are a good case study.

> Then the Lord said to Satan, "Have you considered my servant Job? There is no one on earth like him; he is blameless and upright, a man who fears God and shuns evil."
>
> "Does Job fear God for nothing?" Satan replied. "Have you not put a hedge around him and his household and everything he has? You have blessed the work of his hands, so that his flocks and herds are spread throughout the land. But now stretch out your hand and strike everything he has, and he will surely curse you to your face."
>
> The Lord said to Satan, "Very well, then, everything he has is in your power, but on the man himself do not lay a finger." Then Satan went out from the presence of the Lord.
>
> Job 1:8–12

Satan claims that Job blesses God because God protects Job from evil. But Satan has an experiment he wishes to run. With God's permission, Satan strikes Job's family and possessions. Note how it happens:

> One day when Job's sons and daughters were feasting and drinking wine at the oldest brother's house, a messenger came to Job and said, "The oxen were plowing and the donkeys were grazing nearby, and the Sabeans attacked and made off with them. They put the servants to the sword, and I am the only one who has escaped to tell you!"
>
> While he was still speaking, another messenger came and said, "The fire of God fell from the heavens and burned up the sheep and the servants, and I am the only one who has escaped to tell you!"

While he was still speaking, another messenger came and said, "The Chaldeans formed three raiding parties and swept down on your camels and made off with them. They put the servants to the sword, and I am the only one who has escaped to tell you!" While he was still speaking, yet another messenger came and said, "Your sons and daughters were feasting and drinking wine at the oldest brother's house, when suddenly a mighty wind swept in from the desert and struck the four corners of the house. It collapsed on them and they are dead, and I am the only one who has escaped to tell you!"

Job 1:13–19

Satan strikes Job in several ways. He incites Job's enemies, the Sabeans and the Chaldeans, to kill Job's servants and to steal his animals. Satan uses "the fire of God from heaven"[1] to kill Job's servants and sheep. He also stirs up a "mighty wind" to collapse a building, killing Job's sons and daughters.

From the story, we can assume that, with God's permission, Satan is able to cause all sorts of evil for us as well. He can manipulate natural forces—fire from the sky and wind. Satan also can influence human conflicts and wars. He has the ability to inflict disease, judging from the terrible sickness he gives Job in the next scene: "So Satan went out from the presence of the Lord and afflicted Job with painful sores from the soles of his feet to the crown of his head" (Job 2:7).

It appears that Satan might indeed be the one causing all pain and suffering in the world. But there are a few cautions for us to consider. First, remember that Job's experience is just one among billions of people who have lived on earth. We must be careful not to draw general conclusions from one story. Job's experience does not prove that all the evil things in the world are demonic.

In addition, there are very few incidents in the Bible where demons are clearly responsible for some bad thing that happens. Plenty of evil things are recorded in the Bible, but rarely is the evil explicitly tied to Satan. Most evil in the Bible is connected to sinful humans causing it all.

Don't forget, as well, that Satan is not able to do any of his evil mischief to Job without God's permission. God is sovereign over demonic wickedness. He gives Satan permission to attack Job, but with clear limits.

Does God, then, bring evil into our lives by allowing Satan to do these terrible things? It is a big question, one that is outside of this study. But the question is legitimate: How does God accomplish His will on earth? It appears that He is willing to use Satan and evil in the world to fulfill His purposes.

It is important that we see that God remains in control of His creation. Satan cannot act against God's will. Those of us who are followers of Christ can trust Him with our lives, even when we experience evil and suffering. Here again, Job is a great example for us. He refused to blame God for his pain. He did not understand what he was experiencing, and he surely did not like it. But Job accepted his situation and continued to bless God through it. Job's words to his wife are good advice for all of us who are suffering:

> [Job's] wife said to him, "Are you still maintaining your integrity? Curse God and die!"
>
> He replied, "You are talking like a foolish woman. Shall we accept good from God, and not trouble?" In all this, Job did not sin in what he said.
>
> Job 2:9–10

Satan is powerful. He is able to wreak havoc on the earth. But we who follow Jesus Christ can trust God to see us through any pain and suffering, regardless if it is from Satan or not. We live in a world decimated by sin and evil. To understand the causes is helpful, but that still cannot relieve much of the pain and suffering. God can be trusted with everything in our lives. He promises us that He will be with us all the way through any trials we endure. Our reward is to be with God forever!

The apostle Paul suffered more than most of us to deliver the gospel message to the world. Listen to the hope he offers us all in the midst of suffering:

> Therefore we do not lose heart. Though outwardly we are wasting away, yet inwardly we are being renewed day by day. For our light and momentary troubles are achieving for us an eternal glory that far outweighs them all.
>
> 2 Corinthians 4:16–17

16 If Jesus defeated Satan on the cross, why is Satan still active in the world today?

Japanese Lieutenant Hiroo Onoda refused to give up. During the last year of World War II, Onoda was stationed on the island of Lubang in the Philippines to spy on the American forces there. When he did not receive word that the war had ended, Onoda continued at his post for twenty-nine years. He rejected messages from the Japanese army telling him that the conflict was over. He hid in the jungle in a tattered uniform. It wasn't until 1974 that his former superior officer finally talked him out of hiding and persuaded him to surrender.[1]

Lieutenant Onoda fought the war the best that he could. Evading capture, living off stolen food, he did not stop fighting, even though the war had been over for nearly three decades.

In the spiritual war between God and Satan, the Bible tells us that Jesus Christ defeated Satan 2,000 years ago when He died on the cross. Jesus willingly offered himself as a sacrifice for all sin so that we might be forgiven for all of *our* sin. And with His death,

He broke the power of the devil once and for all, winning the war against sin and evil. The apostle Paul explains:

> When you were dead in your sins . . . , God made you alive with Christ. He forgave us all our sins, having canceled the charge of our legal indebtedness, which stood against us and condemned us; he has taken it away, nailing it to the cross. And having disarmed the powers and authorities, he made a public spectacle of them, triumphing over them by the cross.
>
> Colossians 2:13–15

Paul describes Satan and the demons as powers and authorities conquered by Jesus. What great news! Jesus Christ's death on the cross spells Satan's defeat! Sin's power has been broken. We can be forgiven. The forces of evil have lost. Hallelujah!

Even though Jesus has won the war, the Bible tells us that the spiritual battle continues to this day. Just like Lieutenant Onoda, Satan and his forces continue to fight long after the war has been decided. Why do they press on, causing such misery all over the world? Why does Satan keep fighting?

We cannot know for sure why Satan battles on against God. We would have to be able to get into Satan's mind. But we can piece together enough to at least have an idea why Satan still fights.

Remember that we live today between two great events in this war between God and Satan. The first event is Jesus Christ's death for sin, defeating Satan nearly 2,000 years ago. The second event, though, has not yet taken place. We look forward to Jesus Christ's return to earth in power and glory. On that day, He will banish Satan and the demonic powers once and for all. They will be judged and thrown into hell. At the great last judgment, Jesus will tell all those who do not believe in Him where they are going: "Then [Jesus] will say to those on his left, 'Depart from me, you who are cursed, into the eternal fire prepared for the devil and his angels'" (Matthew 25:41).

The war was decided 2,000 years ago, but the battles continue. Satan won't quit. Casualties build.

So then, in light of the times in which we live, between these two significant events, two possibilities stand out for Satan's continual resistance against God today. One is that Satan simply does not believe the Bible. He believes that he will win the war against God, even though he lost the decisive battle with Jesus long ago.

For you and me, this might sound crazy! How can Satan still believe that he can win? But it's possible that sin has twisted Satan's mind for so long that he may really believe that he is stronger than God. Remember that he had quite an ego problem right from the start, and evil's influence for all these years has corrupted his ability to think sensibly.

A second reason that Satan fights on, even though the war is lost, is that he wants to take as many victims with him as he can before he is banished to hell. Satan's hatred for God runs so deep that he will use everything he's got to doom all the people he can before the end.

Either way, regardless of Satan's motives, it is clear that he is still committed to destroy us. Don't underestimate the power or determination of a doomed foe!

17 Would God ever forgive Satan?

The beauty of the gospel, the good news of Jesus Christ, is that God saves sinners. We all have rebelled against God. But God shows us His love by sending His Son, Jesus, to suffer the penalty for our sin in our place. Humans who are by nature hostile to God are forgiven. There is now peace with God where there was conflict.

He has brought us into His family. It is the greatest reclamation project of all time.

Human beings are not the only creatures who have rebelled against God. Long before, Satan turned against God and led a host of angels in mutiny. They are now under God's condemnation, awaiting the day of judgment. Is there any hope for these fallen angels? Will God ever provide a way for them to be rescued from their doom? Would God ever forgive Satan and the demons?

From the start, we need to admit that we do not know all of God's plans. He never indicates to us that He will fill us in on everything He intends to do. So we need to be careful not to limit God or His forgiveness. What does the Bible contribute to the question?

We find no hope extended to Satan or evil spirits in the Bible. In every case, the Scriptures teach that these fallen spirit-beings are waiting for judgment. They will suffer under God's wrath forever. The horrifying scene is described in the book of Revelation:

> And the devil, who deceived them, was thrown into the lake of burning sulfur, where the beast and the false prophet had been thrown. They will be tormented day and night forever and ever.
>
> Revelation 20:10

The demons know their fate, too. When confronted by Jesus, they fear the time of torment has come: "'What do you want with us, Son of God?' they shouted. 'Have you come here to torture us before the appointed time?'" (Matthew 8:29).

We can speculate that when all the angels were created, they were given a period of time to decide whether they would serve God or rebel against Him. We have no way to know how long ago, or for how long this period extended. But now, from the witness the Scriptures give us, that time of decision has passed. The Bible always shows angels now worshiping God and serving Him perfectly. The Bible always records demons in rebellion, hating God. There simply is no mention of a future angelic rebellion or demonic repentance. There is no hint of forgiveness, reconciliation, or mercy for Satan and the demons. They appear to have crossed a line of no return when they rebelled. So God's judgment is just.

The Bible tells us that human beings have also been given a period of time to decide their fate. Will we turn to God through Jesus Christ or remain rebellious and hostile to God in our sin? Once we die, all decisions appear to be final. The writer of Hebrews makes the point:

> Just as people are destined to die once, and after that to face judgment, so Christ was sacrificed once to take away the sins of many; and he will appear a second time, not to bear sin, but to bring salvation to those who are waiting for him.
>
> Hebrews 9:27–28

The most important question in life confronts us all. Are you forgiven? Have you put your trust in Jesus to take away your sin so that you can experience life with God forever?

If you are not sure, may I ask, "What are you waiting for?" God calls to all of us to come to Him by faith in Jesus Christ, and we will be forgiven. A great old hymn says it well:

> Softly and tenderly Jesus is calling,
> Calling for you and for me;
> See, on the portals He's waiting and watching,
> Watching for you and for me.
>
> Come home, come home,
> You who are weary, come home;
> Earnestly, tenderly, Jesus is calling,
> Calling, O sinner, come home![1]

18 Why does Satan want to destroy us?

We have studied enough Bible passages to be convinced that Satan and the demons dearly desire to harm us. The evil spirits love to harm each of us individually with physical and mental torment. They also wish to gain control of us to further harass us. The demons also seek to stir up conflict, strife, and division among us as a human race. War is their delight!

Satan's ultimate goal is to see human beings die spiritually, forever separated from God's love and kindness.

Why is Satan so dedicated to destroying us? Why do we seem to matter so much to him? The Bible never really spells out an answer. But we can bring together a few biblical ideas to construct a good theory to explain Satan's hatred for us and his desire to destroy us.

First, the Bible makes it clear that Satan despises God. He hates God and everything that God is by nature—loving, kind, merciful, pure, etc. Satan is the opposite. His pride and vanity consume him. His rebellion against God has warped and twisted him into a being who by nature is hateful, mean, vengeful, and cruel. When Jesus squared off with His opponents, listen to what He said about them, and about Satan:

> You belong to your father, the devil, and you want to carry out your father's desires. He was a murderer from the beginning, not holding to the truth, for there is no truth in him. When he lies, he speaks his native language, for he is a liar and the father of lies.
>
> John 8:44

Since God loves us, Satan hates us. He is dedicated to destroying us.

The Bible also teaches us that we as a human race are created in the image of God:

> Then God said, "Let us make mankind in our image, in our likeness, so that they may rule over the fish in the sea and the birds in the sky, over the livestock and all the wild animals, and over all the creatures that move along the ground."
> So God created mankind in his own image,
>   in the image of God he created them;
>   male and female he created them.
>
> Genesis 1:26–27

We are special, unique, to be created in God's image. No other creature in the Bible, including the angels, is called the image of God. In God's image, the human race reflects God in who we are—intelligent, loving, and creative. Our relationship with God is also unique. Jesus came to die for human sinners, not demons or any other creature. Human beings also are given a unique task to accomplish. God told the first humans that they had a lofty role to fill on earth:

> God blessed them and said to them, "Be fruitful and increase in number; fill the earth and subdue it. Rule over the fish in the sea and the birds in the sky and over every living creature that moves on the ground."
>
> Genesis 1:28

We alone are given dominion over the earth, to rule over every animal on earth.

Because we bear God's image, we have a target on our backs. Satan cannot harm God himself, but he can bring harm to God's image bearers. Assaulting God's image is an attack on God. Satan can grieve God by corrupting His creation.

On the other hand, we can bring glory to the Creator by coming to Him in faith, through Jesus Christ, for the forgiveness of sins. We can know God, assuming our intended role as God's image, loving and serving Him with a full heart. Satan's wrath against us is turned to great glory and joy through Jesus Christ!

19 If I ignore Satan, will he go away or just leave me alone?

Satan has declared war on the human race. He hates God and seeks to destroy God's creatures, with humans at the top of his hit list. Fear might drive some of us into denial. "If I just don't think about Satan, he will leave me alone." We might also think that if we refuse to take the side of God or Satan, we will be able to stay out of the conflict. Can we avoid Satan's attacks by ignoring him? Can we remain neutral in this spiritual war?

The Bible tells us that Satan's attacks are real. Therefore, we cannot ignore him or his assaults. The apostle Peter tells us what we are up against: "Be alert and of sober mind. Your enemy the devil prowls around like a roaring lion looking for someone to devour" (1 Peter 5:8).

We are to remain on the alert and treat Satan's attacks as serious. We cannot shrink back in fear, refusing to recognize the danger. To ignore the devil is like a fearful child who covers his eyes and turns away from the threat, hoping that his actions will make the danger go away. All he has done is to make himself even more vulnerable.

Can we call a truce with the devil, pledging not to follow Jesus Christ if Satan will leave us alone? Nothing in the Bible gives the slightest hope to anyone who tries to stay out of it all. Because we have been created in God's image, Satan is determined to destroy us. We are in a war, and this enemy doesn't stop his attacks until he destroys us, regardless of what we do.

Peter goes on to reassure those who follow Jesus Christ of God's protection:

> Resist [the devil], standing firm in the faith, because you know that the family of believers throughout the world is undergoing the same kind of sufferings. And the God of all grace, who called you to his eternal glory in Christ, after you have suffered a little while, will himself restore you and make you strong, firm and steadfast. To him be the power forever and ever. Amen.
>
> 1 Peter 5:9–11

The challenge for us is to take our stand with the Lord Jesus Christ against Satan. There is no safer way to face the devil's hate.

20 How do I know if Satan is really attacking me or not?

Life at times looks like a long series of trials, difficulties, struggles, and obstacles. Nothing seems to go right! If we expressed this out loud, it might sound like, "I feel as if the whole world is ganging up against me!"

Not only in these low moments, but for life in general, how much are demons causing our problems? Two extreme answers to the question emerge. Some people see every setback as caused by demons. They believe, quite literally, that there is a demon under every rock. Others don't think about spiritual warfare at all. The problems they experience are a result of bad luck, poor choices, mistakes, or the ill will of others.

So what's the real story? It's probably somewhere between the two extremes. The Bible helps set a good perspective on demonic attacks. To be sure, the Scriptures record several incidents of attacks by evil spirits. These events are direct, clear-cut spiritual encounters. However, most passages that address trials do not mention Satan at all. The devil might be involved in more than what is mentioned, but the New Testament identifies other factors that contribute to our struggles. One major cause is our old, fallen human nature. The Bible is clear. All humans are born rebellious against God. The apostle Paul put himself in the same boat as all humanity before he became a follower of Jesus Christ:

> All of us also lived among [the disobedient] at one time, gratifying the cravings of our flesh and following its desires and thoughts. Like the rest, we were by nature deserving of wrath.
>
> Ephesians 2:3

Paul talks about this old nature as our flesh. Sin is not something we have to try very hard to do. We come by it easily. Just by being ourselves, we buck against God. Even after we make peace with God and become a follower of Christ, the old nature sticks around:

> So I say, walk by the [Holy] Spirit, and you will not gratify the desires of the flesh. For the flesh desires what is contrary to the Spirit, and the Spirit what is contrary to the flesh. They are in conflict with each other, so that you are not to do whatever you want.
>
> Galatians 5:16–17

The battle rages between the Holy Spirit (God) and the flesh (our old sinful nature). It appears Satan does not have to do too much. We bring all kinds of difficulties upon ourselves all by ourselves.

The apostle John adds more to our understanding of what causes our trials in life. All of us humans together create an environment set against God:

> Do not love the world or anything in the world. If anyone loves the world, love for the Father is not in them. For everything in the world—the lust of the flesh, the lust of the eyes, and the pride of life—comes not from the Father but from the world.
>
> 1 John 2:15–16

The "world" is the human race's way of thinking. It includes all manner of selfishness, corruption, manipulation, and cravings.

Satan certainly can and does add his wicked powers to what we create ourselves as sinful humans. How should we respond, then? First, it is always a good thing to take everything to God. He offers His protective care against Satan for all those who are followers of Christ. Jesus Christ is Lord over all spiritual forces! As James said, "Submit yourselves, then, to God. Resist the devil, and he will flee from you. Come near to God and he will come near to you" (4:7–8).

Second, we need to avoid becoming paranoid about Satan's attacks while keeping our eyes alert for potential spiritual forces at work in our situation. Remember that we can bring all of these matters to God. Just talk to Him about everything, and trust Him to help you. A great old hymn says it well:

> What a friend we have in Jesus,
> All our sins and griefs to bear!
> What a privilege to carry
> Everything to God in prayer!
>
> Oh, what peace we often forfeit,
> Oh, what needless pain we bear,
> All because we do not carry
> Everything to God in prayer!
>
> Have we trials and temptations?
> Is there trouble anywhere?
> We should never be discouraged—
> Take it to the Lord in prayer.
>
> Can we find a friend so faithful,
> Who will all our sorrows share?
> Jesus knows our every weakness;
> Take it to the Lord in prayer.[1]

21 How do I stand firm against Satan?

What the Bible tells us about the devil is pretty scary. Satan is powerful. He hates us and wants to destroy us. How do we survive this? Is there any hope? We are lost if we think that we can take on Satan and the evil spirits by ourselves.

Thankfully, the Scriptures assure us of God's protection when we become followers of Jesus Christ. The apostle Paul says it best:

> For I am convinced that neither death nor life, neither angels nor demons, neither the present nor the future, nor any powers, neither height nor depth, nor anything else in all creation, will be able to separate us from the love of God that is in Christ Jesus our Lord.
>
> Romans 8:38–39

That just about settles it! We are permanently connected to the love of God through Christ. Nothing is able to break that bond!

The Bible makes it clear, however, that we must also act to protect ourselves against the devil. We cannot sit back and wait for God to do it all. Or worse, we cannot dabble in demonic activities and expect God to bail us out based on these verses.

Paul urges all followers of Christ to take measures against Satan and the demons:

> Finally, be strong in the Lord and in his mighty power. Put on the full armor of God, so that you can take your stand against the devil's schemes. For our struggle is not against flesh and blood, but against the rulers, against the authorities, against the powers of this dark world and against the spiritual forces of evil in the heavenly realms. Therefore put on the full armor of God, so that when the

day of evil comes, you may be able to stand your ground, and after you have done everything, to stand.

Ephesians 6:10–13

Paul helps us to see beyond the obvious to the warfare waged in the heavenly realms against spiritual forces, not just human adversaries. God is our strength. His mighty power and full armor allow us to stand our ground against the devil. We do not run away, buckle under the pressure, or give in. Paul tells us to take our stand, not in our own strength, but with the power of God working for us against Satan.

Think of a young girl chased into her room by a mischievous older brother. She closes the door, but her brother is stronger than she is, and the door begins to give way. Suddenly, a firm hand and arm appear over the girl's head to push the door closed with far more strength than her brother possesses. She looks back to see her father smiling at her with love shining in his eyes.

God's love for us gives us the power to hold back Satan. We are safe with God holding the door against Satan. Paul gives us even more clarity to see how we stand firm against the devil:

Stand firm then, with the belt of truth buckled around your waist, with the breastplate of righteousness in place, and with your feet fitted with the readiness that comes from the gospel of peace. In addition to all this, take up the shield of faith, with which you can extinguish all the flaming arrows of the evil one. Take the helmet of salvation and the sword of the Spirit, which is the word of God. And pray in the Spirit on all occasions with all kinds of prayers and requests. With this in mind, be alert and always keep on praying for all the Lord's people.

Ephesians 6:14–18

God's armor protects us when we battle Satan. Notice two of these pieces of armor. First, God's Word, the Bible, gives us all the protection we need against Satan's temptations. Jesus is our example, fending off Satan's lures with Scripture quotations:

> Then Jesus was led by the Spirit into the wilderness to be tempted by the devil. After fasting forty days and forty nights, he was hungry. The tempter came to him and said, "If you are the Son of God, tell these stones to become bread."
>
> Jesus answered, "It is written: 'Man shall not live on bread alone, but on every word that comes from the mouth of God.'"
>
> Matthew 4:1–4

Two more times that day the devil tempted Jesus, and He quoted Scripture both times to fend off Satan's attacks. We can learn from Jesus. We don't argue with Satan or get into long debates. We use the Bible to answer the evil one. The Bible is a sharp and dangerous sword against evil powers. We do well to read it, study it, memorize it, reflect on its meaning, and proclaim it.

Second, Paul urges us to bring every concern to God "with all kinds of prayers and requests," both for ourselves and for our Christian brothers and sisters. We talk to God about everything. If Satan tempts us, we turn to our Father. God walks right with us, and His power is available all the time if we ask for it.

As we follow Jesus Christ, we can don the armor of God to fend off Satan's attacks. It is there for the asking. We can trust God to take care of us against this evil foe. Stand firm against the dark powers!

22 Do demons inhabit specific places?

Ghosts are a part of American culture almost as much as baseball and apple pie. Polls in the last decade indicate that anywhere from one-third to a majority of Americans believe in ghosts.[1] Haunted houses and spirits roaming the earth are part of headline news and popular entertainment.

Along with belief in ghosts, many people, including followers of Jesus Christ, also believe that demons haunt specific places—houses, church buildings, cities, and even whole nations. For example, church leaders are called into a home to cleanse it from evil spirits causing trouble. Is there anything to it? Do demons really live in specific places?

The Bible has a little evidence for these resident spirits. For example, the angel Gabriel informs the prophet Daniel of spiritual battles he wages with the "prince of Persia" and the "prince of Greece" (Daniel 10:20). The apostle Paul in his letters also refers to "rulers, authorities, powers, and forces" (Ephesians 6:12) in the heavens, perhaps signifying that these evil spirits live in designated places.

A quick scan of the Internet reveals many Christian organizations that claim to be deliverance ministries. They advertise their ability to deliver people from satanic oppression and possession. Most of them also teach that demons dwell in specific locations, creating all sorts of evil for humans who venture into their territory. These "territorial spirits"[2] cause sin and suffering in the same location year after year if they are not evicted. It's as if these demons haunt specific places.

It is the purpose of deliverance ministries to identify and expel the resident demons. To identify demonic powers, some ministries practice "spiritual mapping"—discovering spiritual bondage and evil spirits present as a result of past sin or evil in a specific location.[3] Once demonic forces are located, Christians are instructed to pray against these powers in Jesus Christ's name to compel them to leave the area.[4] Once the evil forces are gone, God's work in the area can bloom.

Our response to the claims of these deliverance ministries should be cautious. On the one hand, the Bible opens the door to the existence of territorial spirits stationed in various places on earth. However, the Scriptures never teach that we should aggressively seek out these demons to expel them. There is only a thin connection that can be made in one of Paul's letters. After he exhorts the Ephesian Christians to stand firm against these forces of evil, Paul concludes with this instruction: "And pray in the Spirit on all occasions with all kinds of prayers and requests. With this in mind, be alert and always keep on praying for all the Lord's people" (Ephesians 6:18).

The prayers are directed to God for the Lord's people, not against satanic powers.

When Paul traveled from city to city spreading the good news of Christ, he never sought out evil spirits entrenched in the area. He always proclaimed Christ. If he came into contact with demons, he dealt with them. But he never went out looking for them.

We need to be open to the possibility that demons live in particular places on earth. We also need to focus on God and the gospel of Jesus Christ. Any reports of demonic haunting must be treated with great care and discernment. And when we are faced with clear demonic powers manifesting themselves in people, we need to confront them in the power of the Lord Jesus Christ.

23 Should I worry about demons attacking me?

All across the world people live in dread of evil spirits, especially those who are animists. Animists believe that all of nature—rocks, trees, rivers, etc.—is inhabited with spirits. Many of the spirits are hostile to humans. People must take action to placate the spirits through sacrifices, prayers, and other offerings.[1]

The Bible teaches that, indeed, there are many malicious spirits dedicated to our destruction. This realization leaves people with anxiety similar to those of animists: "I am afraid of Satan! He is out to get me." Several legitimate questions come from these anxieties, such as "Should I be worried about Satan and demons attacking me and my loved ones?"

The Scriptures respond both yes and no. Yes, we all should be concerned about demon attacks. Satan and his host really do hate us. They *are* out to get us. Unprotected, we stand little chance against such an imposing foe. We need to face that reality soberly.

But on the other hand, no, we have no reason to fear demons if we belong to Jesus Christ. As powerful and evil as Satan is, God is the one who calls the shots. And evil spirits know it. James helps us to understand in his short letter: "You believe that there is one God. Good! Even the demons believe that—and shudder" (James 2:19).

The apostle Peter reassures us of God's protection against Satan:

> Cast all your anxiety on him because he cares for you. Be alert and of sober mind. Your enemy the devil prowls around like a roaring lion looking for someone to devour. Resist him, standing firm in the faith, because you know that the family of believers throughout the world is undergoing the same kind of sufferings. And the God of all grace, who called you to his eternal glory in Christ, after you have

71

suffered a little while, will himself restore you and make you strong, firm and steadfast. To him be the power for ever and ever. Amen.

1 Peter 5:7–11

The apostle Paul tells us that God relieves all our worries when we bring them to Him:

Do not be anxious about anything, but in every situation, by prayer and petition, with thanksgiving, present your requests to God. And the peace of God, which transcends all understanding, will guard your hearts and your minds in Christ Jesus.

Philippians 4:6–7

Best of all, the Lord Jesus Christ comforts us with the promise He gave the night before He died. His followers were worried when Jesus told them that He was leaving them. But Jesus gave them, and us, something to believe in: "I have told you these things, so that in me you may have peace. In this world you will have trouble. But take heart! I have overcome the world" (John 16:33).

The resurrected Christ stands by all those who belong to Him. We have nothing to fear as long as we keep following right behind the King, the Lord Jesus Christ.

24 Do demons have specific names that describe their roles, like a demon of lust, greed, lying, etc.?

Not long ago, a series of novels stirred up interest in angels, demons, and spiritual warfare. *This Present Darkness*, written by Frank Peretti in 1986, got people thinking about the unseen conflict between God and Satan. A prominent feature of his stories is that all of the spiritual beings, both good and evil, have names. Some are proper names, like Tal and Rafar. Some of the demons have labels for names, such as Madness and Witchcraft.[1] Is this just a fictional part of Peretti's story, or do demons really have specific names?

It is reasonable to assume that all angels and demons have names because they are personal beings. God created angels with the ability to think, express emotions, and make choices. All of these creatures may have names for themselves. Very few angel and demon names are actually given in the Bible, however. Michael and Gabriel are the only angels who are named. The names of evil spirits are unclear, except for Satan himself. For example, Beelzebul is a name given to the prince of demons by the Jews of Jesus' time (Matthew 12:24). Apparently, it is another name for Satan, since there is no evidence that this is another demon. When demons are loosed on the earth in the book of Revelation, John describes their chief: "They had as king over them the angel of the Abyss, whose name in Hebrew is Abaddon and in Greek is Apollyon (that is, Destroyer)" (Revelation 9:11).

This creature is called an angel, but his name means "destroyer," hardly a name for one of God's good angels. As king over the demons, is Abbadon yet another name for Satan? The Scriptures are inconclusive.

The most direct illustration of a name for an evil spirit is in the gospel of Mark. Jesus confronted a demonized man: "Then Jesus asked him, 'What is your name?' 'My name is Legion,' he replied, 'for we are many'" (Mark 5:9).

The name for this demon may be merely a description, not a proper name. A Roman legion consisted of 6,000 men.[2] Thousands of demons might have been tormenting this poor man, with *Legion* used to drive home the point.

Jesus also dealt with a demonized boy who couldn't speak or hear. Note what Jesus said when He addressed the demon: "When

Jesus saw that a crowd was running to the scene, he rebuked the impure spirit. 'You deaf and mute spirit,' he said, 'I command you, come out of him and never enter him again'" (Mark 9:25).

We cannot be sure if Jesus labeled the demon with the name "deaf and mute," or whether He used these two words to describe the kind of control the demon had over the boy. The scriptural evidence is inconclusive.

There are a large number of testimonials from Christian deliverance ministries that claim to discover names for evil spirits such as Greed, Envy, or Murder. These claims must be evaluated carefully. We must note, however, that very little evidence from the Bible supports these testimonies. The Bible lists greed, envy, and murder as some of the sins that we humans commit without much demonic help:

> The acts of the flesh are obvious: sexual immorality, impurity and debauchery; idolatry and witchcraft; hatred, discord, jealousy, fits of rage, selfish ambition, dissensions, factions and envy; drunkenness, orgies, and the like. I warn you, as I did before, that those who live like this will not inherit the kingdom of God.
>
> Galatians 5:19–21

In the wisdom of God, He chooses to withhold from us the specific names of most angels and demons. We may conclude that the subject is not something that we must know to follow God effectively, despite our curiosity, or God would have included it in the Bible.

25 Are some demons more powerful than others?

Author C. S. Lewis may be more popular today than when he lived over fifty years ago. His fiction captures the imaginations of readers as he grapples with important themes. One of his lesser-known fictional books is *The Screwtape Letters*. As the story goes, Lewis intercepts a series of letters between two demons, Screwtape and Wormwood. Screwtape offers instruction to help Wormwood keep his "patient"—his human subject—from belief in God. Lewis's insight into human nature, sin, and temptation from a demonic perspective gives us much to think about.

One feature of *The Screwtape Letters* is the apparent rank of demons in Satan's service. It becomes clear that Screwtape is higher ranking than Wormwood, but other demons are authorities over Screwtape. It raises several questions. Do the dark powers work together against humans? Are some demons more powerful than others? Is there a ranking of evil spirits?

Several Bible passages indicate that some demons hold high rank. Of course, Satan is the highest over all evil spirits. Jesus tells us that hell itself was not created for humans but for the devil and his angels (Matthew 25:41).

Some evil spirits are more powerful than the rest, because they take more effort to cast out, according to Jesus in Mark's gospel: "This [spirit] can come out only by prayer" (Mark 9:29).

There also appear to be high-ranking demons who oversee evil in entire nations. For example, when the angel Gabriel meets the prophet Daniel, Gabriel explains why he was delayed in coming:

> Do not be afraid, Daniel. Since the first day that you set your mind to gain understanding and to humble yourself before your God,

your words were heard, and I have come in response to them. But the prince of the Persian kingdom resisted me twenty-one days. Then Michael, one of the chief princes, came to help me, because I was detained there with the king of Persia.

Daniel 10:12–13

Gabriel lets us see into a conflict that is usually hidden from us. He and the angel Michael fight against the high demonic power over the nation of Persia. A few verses later, Gabriel continues to explain things to Daniel:

Do you know why I have come to you? Soon I will return to fight against the prince of Persia, and when I go, the prince of Greece will come; but first I will tell you what is written in the Book of Truth. (No one supports me against them except Michael, your prince.)

Daniel 10:20–21

The spiritual battle extends to include the evil spirit over Greece as well. These demons appear to have greater power than most other demons.

The apostle Paul supports a higher ranking for some demons in a few of his letters. For example, Paul warns those who followed Christ in Ephesus against these powers:

For our struggle is not against flesh and blood, but against the rulers, against the authorities, against the powers of this dark world and against the spiritual forces of evil in the heavenly realms.

Ephesians 6:12

Paul uses four expressions to describe these evil spirits. They are *rulers*, *authorities*, *powers*, and *forces of evil*. It is clear that these are spiritual beings because Paul referred to them as being "in the heavenly realms." The heavens are the place where God and spirit-beings normally dwell.

We can conclude from this biblical evidence that there must be a hierarchy of demonic powers that rule in some respect under Satan.

Our awareness of these greater and lesser demonic forces appears to be limited. Our response should be consistent, regardless of the authority or power of a demon. No demonic presence should be underestimated in our determination to resist Satan and his host. All demons are serious threats to the human race, especially if we downplay their influence in our lives.

26 Does God control what demons can do?

When we study spiritual warfare in the Bible, two truths stand out. One is about Satan and evil spirits. They are active, deceptive, and relentless. Satan uses many tactics to bring us down.

The other truth is about God. He is sovereign, which means that He rules the universe. God controls all rule, authority, and power, including the forces of Satan and his host.

Does God enforce any limits on Satan, then? How much freedom does the devil have to attack us? To begin with, Satan and the demons have broad permission to tempt us. The first instance is in the Garden of Eden in Genesis. Satan is allowed to interact with Eve, tempting her to doubt God's words. God easily could have erected a barrier to keep the serpent away from Eve. It would have been the first restraining order in history!

Two other Bible texts help us to understand Satan's freedom and his limits. The first is in the first two chapters of Job. Satan wants to harm Job to find out if Job really loves God regardless of his circumstances:

> "Does Job fear God for nothing?" Satan replied. "Have you not put a hedge around him and his household and everything he has? You

have blessed the work of his hands, so that his flocks and herds are spread throughout the land. But now stretch out your hand and strike everything he has, and he will surely curse you to your face."

The Lord said to Satan, "Very well, then, everything he has is in your power, but on the man himself do not lay a finger." Then Satan went out from the presence of the Lord.

Job 1:9–12

God permits Satan to strike everything Job has, but with a clear limit. Satan may not harm Job himself. In the next scene, after Job passes the first test, Satan speaks with God again:

"Skin for skin!" Satan replied. "A man will give all he has for his own life. But now stretch out your hand and strike [Job's] flesh and bones, and he will surely curse you to your face."

The Lord said to Satan, "Very well, then, he is in your hands; but you must spare his life." So Satan went out from the presence of the Lord and afflicted Job with painful sores from the soles of his feet to the crown of his head.

Job 2:4–7

Once again, Satan harms Job only as much as God specifies. God remains in complete control of the situation, but Satan also is loosed on Job like an attack dog.

Another passage written centuries later allows us to see the same pattern. The evil King Ahab allies with King Jehoshaphat to attack a neighboring country. Even though Ahab is a rebellious king, he seeks out prophets to find out if God wishes them to proceed with the attack. Every prophet but one tells Ahab that God will give him success in the battle. Only the prophet Micaiah warns Ahab against war. Micaiah relays a remarkable vision of heaven that he saw:

Therefore hear the word of the Lord: I saw the Lord sitting on his throne with all the multitudes of heaven standing around him on his right and on his left. And the Lord said, "Who will entice Ahab into attacking Ramoth Gilead and going to his death there?"

One suggested this, and another that. Finally, a spirit came forward, stood before the Lord and said, "I will entice him."

"By what means?" the Lord asked.

"I will go out and be a deceiving spirit in the mouths of all his prophets," he said.

"You will succeed in enticing him," said the Lord. "Go and do it." So now the Lord has put a deceiving spirit in the mouths of all these prophets of yours. The Lord has decreed disaster for you.

1 Kings 22:19–23

Both angels and demons have gathered around God in the vision. Apparently an evil spirit suggests a plan to deceive all of the other prophets. God endorses the tactic and commands the spirit to carry it out. Ahab's evil reign is finished, and his day of reckoning has come.

We learn in this story that God may, at times, use demonic powers to accomplish His purposes. The evil powers wish to harm humans any way they can, so God uses their hatred for His own ends.

What does all of this mean for us as followers of Jesus Christ? Will God protect us from Satan or not? The Bible is clear that God will always act in our best interests. He will protect us, but sometimes He uses trials and difficulties to help us to grow into mature, godly followers of Christ. It appears that even Satan's actions against a follower of Christ may be used by God to bring good into the person's life. The apostle Paul illustrates. He speaks about wonderful, secret visions of heaven that he saw, but with a difficult result:

Therefore, in order to keep me from becoming conceited, I was given a thorn in my flesh, a messenger of Satan, to torment me. Three times I pleaded with the Lord to take it away from me. But he said to me, "My grace is sufficient for you, for my power is made perfect in weakness." Therefore I will boast all the more gladly about my weaknesses, so that Christ's power may rest on me. That is why, for Christ's sake, I delight in weaknesses, in insults, in hardships, in persecutions, in difficulties. For when I am weak, then I am strong.

2 Corinthians 12:7–10

God used Satan's attack on Paul to keep Paul humble and dependent on His power. Despite the hardships, Paul was glad to grow closer to God. We, too, can trust God in all that we experience in life—pleasures and trials. God gives us no guarantee against demonic attacks, but He will always protect us. He also will use everything that comes into our lives for good: "And we know that in all things God works for the good of those who love him, who have been called according to his purpose" (Romans 8:28).

We may not see the good in our experiences at the time, but we trust God to care for us far more than we can imagine.

27 Is it possible to actually see demons?

Human beings are, by nature, emotional creatures. We are easily influenced by feelings, intuition, premonitions, and gut impressions of what is going on around us. For example, some places feel evil. Just recently, I visited the ruins of Terezin, a Nazi concentration camp in northern Czechoslovakia during World War II. Several rooms that had warehoused prisoners like cattle carried an emotional weight that defies description. Almost seventy years after the war ended, I still felt the wickedness of the place—human beings suffering in appalling conditions. And there were Nazi camps far worse than Terezin.

Is it possible that there is an evil spiritual presence adding to the human wickedness in places like Terezin? Are we sometimes able to see demons or feel their presence?

The Bible speaks about the traffic between the spiritual domain of existence and the physical universe. The Bible begins, "In the beginning God created the heavens and the earth." The heavens are the home to all spiritual beings—God himself, His angels, Satan, and the demons. God also created the earth and the entire physical universe. He created human beings in His image and gave us dominion over the earth.

We learn in the Bible that God's angels appear on earth on special missions. The birth of Jesus Christ included angels appearing to humans and speaking with them. For instance, the angel Gabriel visited Mary and told her that she was pregnant with "the Son of the Most High" (Luke 1:32). Months later, when Jesus was born, an angel spoke to shepherds in the fields outside of Bethlehem:

> And there were shepherds living out in the fields nearby, keeping watch over their flocks at night. An angel of the Lord appeared to them, and the glory of the Lord shone around them, and they were terrified. But the angel said to them, "Do not be afraid. I bring you good news that will cause great joy for all the people. Today in the town of David a Savior has been born to you; he is the Messiah, the Lord."
>
> Luke 2:8–11

The passage shows that the shepherds saw the angel and heard him speak.

Demons are angels who have been corrupted by evil. Can they, too, appear to people? Can we see, hear, or feel the presence of demons? Many testimonies circulate confirming demon sightings. The reports vary widely, but they have common details. Some of the stories run parallel with popular Christian fiction, as well. Author Frank Peretti includes vivid descriptions of demons in his novels. They appear with bulging yellow eyes, bat wings, fangs, and breathing sulfur. Testimonies consistent with these descriptions are numerous and substantial. They draw our attention to the real possibility of demon manifestations.

The picture changes when we look at the witness of Scripture. The Bible never depicts a demon manifesting itself in tangible ways like angels do. In Bible times, demonic appearances on earth are through evil spirits infesting humans.

Does this mean that those who claim to see demons today are deceived? Not necessarily. However, any experience that we claim to have that goes beyond what the Bible teaches must be approached with great caution. For those of us who follow Christ, the challenge is to discipline ourselves to bring all of our experiences to the Bible for evaluation. Otherwise we might fall into the danger of promoting superstition, folklore, and rumors that take us away from God's truth revealed in the Bible.

28 Just how many demons are there?

The Bible teaches us that Satan and demons are declared enemies of the human race. They seek to destroy us. Their tactics are clever. They are relentless. We are in serious danger if demons set out to assault us. But are there enough demons to attack every person on earth? Do we find safety in numbers? Just how many demons are there?

The short answer is "We do not know!" There is no official demon census taken every ten years. The Bible does not give us a solid figure for the number of demons, either. We are not able to count spiritual beings, whom we cannot even see if they wish to remain hidden to us.

The Bible does give us some clues, however, to the number of evil spirits. Demons are former angels who rebelled against God. We know that there are many angels yet today who never sinned. When Jesus was being arrested just before His trial, His followers tried to defend Him with weapons. Jesus assured them that He had plenty of help available from angels if He needed it: "Do you think I cannot call on my Father, and he will at once put at my disposal more than twelve legions of angels?" (Matthew 26:53).

In Jesus' time, a Roman legion of soldiers consisted of 6,000 troops.[1] Jesus claims more than 72,000 angels at His personal disposal. And there may be many more serving God in other ways, too.

The Bible hints that there may be fewer demons than angels (Revelation 12:4, 9). Jesus helps us, however, to understand that there are quite a large number of demons (Mark 5:9). Jesus also says that angels and demons are not able to reproduce like humans do. When we get to heaven, we no longer marry and have children: "When the dead rise, they will neither marry nor be given in marriage; they will be like the angels in heaven" (Mark 12:25).

God seems to have created a specific number of angels, and they cannot reproduce themselves. The number of demons appears to be the same for all time. Are there enough demons to tempt every person on earth? There are over seven billion (and counting) people on earth. If each person has a corresponding demon to tempt them, that is a lot of demons!

Even if there are more people alive on earth today than there are demons to tempt them, it should not give us any comfort to try to find safety in numbers. Satan is intelligent enough to direct his forces to assault humans according to his plans. We cannot know what those plans are, so caution tells us to be ready to stand firm against demonic attacks at all times.

29 Why did Jesus forbid demons from speaking when He cast them out?

When He walked the earth, Jesus demonstrated His authority over demons when He encountered them. There was never any doubt. The evil spirits did exactly what Jesus commanded them to do. On several occasions, Jesus told the spirits to be quiet when He cast them out of someone. For example, the gospel writer Luke describes a scene in a Jewish place of worship:

> In the synagogue there was a man possessed by a demon, an impure spirit. He cried out at the top of his voice, "Go away! What do you want with us, Jesus of Nazareth? Have you come to destroy us? I know who you are—the Holy One of God!"
> "Be quiet!" Jesus said sternly. "Come out of him!" Then the demon threw the man down before them all and came out without injuring him.
>
> Luke 4:33–35

Later in the same day, Luke reports Jesus' encounters with many dark spirits.

> Moreover, demons came out of many people, shouting, "You are the Son of God!" But [Jesus] rebuked them and would not allow them to speak, because they knew he was the Messiah.
>
> Luke 4:41

Why did Jesus order the evil spirits to be quiet? Was there some important reason that He silenced these demons? The purpose for Jesus' action is never explained to us in the Bible, so all we can do is take an educated guess. It may be as simple as bringing order to

84

a chaotic scene. When demons manifested themselves in people, the situation was usually charged. Demonized people were often violent. When they saw Jesus, they screamed or shouted under the demons' control. Silencing the demons probably lowered the tension in the room immediately.

Quieting the demons also clearly revealed to everyone that Jesus had authority over the evil spirits. He commanded, and they stopped speaking right away.

A third possibility for Jesus' stifling the demons may come from what the demons were saying when Jesus approached. They shouted, "You are the Holy One of God," or "You are the Son of God." Jesus did not wish for people to learn who He was from dark spirits. He did not need or want demonic testimony to support His claim to be God's Son. The same possibility surfaced years later when the apostle Paul proclaimed the gospel in the town of Philippi. Luke reports Paul's encounter with a demonized girl:

> She followed Paul and the rest of us, shouting, "These men are servants of the Most High God, who are telling you the way to be saved." She kept this up for many days. Finally Paul became so annoyed that he turned around and said to the spirit, "In the name of Jesus Christ I command you to come out of her!" At that moment the spirit left her.
>
> Acts 16:17–18

Paul acted to keep things clear. He and his companions proclaimed Jesus Christ so that people would believe in Jesus and be saved. He saw this demon testimony as a distraction. It also might confuse people about who Jesus and Paul were. They were not sent from demons, but from God himself.

We do not know for sure why Jesus and Paul silenced demons. We *do* know that Jesus commands all of His followers never to stop talking about Him and the gospel: "[Jesus] said to [His followers], 'Go into all the world and preach the gospel to all creation'" (Mark 16:15).

30 Do bad people become demons when they die?

One of the most delightful movies shown at Christmas is Frank Capra's *It's a Wonderful Life*. It premiered in December 1946. The film's hero, George Bailey, is facing a crisis in his life. He is on the verge of suicide. But he discovers that his life is not a failure through the help of Clarence Oddbody, an "angel" sent from heaven. Clarence shows George all the good he has brought into the world throughout his life. George learns that his life is truly wonderful.

As part of the story, we learn that Clarence lived two hundred years earlier, died, and went to heaven to become an angel. Clarence now is trying to "earn his wings" by coming to George's aid.

It's a Wonderful Life plays on a widespread belief that good people become angels when they die. But if that's true, what about bad people when they die? Do they become evil angels?

As with many beliefs about angels and demons, folklore runs far ahead of truth. Despite all of the stories, the Bible offers no hint to suggest that good people who die become angels and bad people become demons. Human beings are completely different creatures from angels or demons, and always remain that way.

The Bible helps us to understand who and what angels are. In the book of Hebrews in the New Testament, we learn several things about angels:

> Are not all angels ministering spirits sent to serve those who will inherit salvation?
>
> Hebrews 1:14

Do not forget to show hospitality to strangers, for by so doing some people have shown hospitality to angels without knowing it.

Hebrews 13:2

Angels are spirit-beings, not humans. They possess the ability to appear to us as normal human beings if they wish, but they are not humans. So it follows, too, that demons are not evil people who have died. There is no wicked demon today, for example, who lived as Adolf Hitler until he died in 1945, and then became a demon. Evil spirits are creatures distinct from us.

When people die, their bodies are buried, but they live on as spirit-beings in heaven or hell. But they are human spirits, not angelic spirits. The Bible teaches that a day is coming when humans who have died will receive new bodies that will never die:

Listen, I tell you a mystery: We will not all [die], but we will all be changed—in a flash, in the twinkling of an eye, at the last trumpet. For the trumpet will sound, the dead will be raised imperishable, and we will be changed.

1 Corinthians 15:51–52

Those who died as followers of Jesus Christ will be raised to life as immortal human beings. Those who died apart from Christ will be raised to punishment at the last judgment.

We can still enjoy the stories about people becoming angels as long as we treat them as what they are: fictional tales to entertain us. Little of the folklore is rooted in fact.

31 Are other religions' idols really controlled by demons?

The world of the Bible was much different from our world today. In both Old Testament times and the New Testament years, religions of all types dominated the globe. Judaism and Christianity were born in a world filled with gods and idols. Rather than believing in many gods, or polytheism, Jews and Christians affirm one God only. It set Israel apart from the neighboring nations. It made Christianity an oddity in the Roman world that conceived it. The ancient world was filled with gods and idols fashioned to represent them.

The Old Testament Scriptures affirm only one God. He made himself known to Abraham, appeared to Moses, and through Moses formed the nation of Israel as His people. And at the core of Israel's faith, Judaism, was the declaration that there is only one God: "Hear, O Israel: The Lord our God, the Lord is one" (Deuteronomy 6:4).

Next to the God of Israel, every other god is nothing. All through the Old Testament, God disproves the claims of other nations about the power of their gods. One passage describes a confrontation between the God of Israel and Baal, a competing god. A test was given to each god. After an animal sacrifice was prepared, both gods were summoned by their followers to send fire from heaven to burn up the sacrifice. When the prophets of Baal called out to Baal, nothing happened:

> Then they called on the name of Baal from morning till noon. "Baal, answer us!" they shouted. But there was no response; no one answered. And they danced around the altar they had made.

At noon Elijah began to taunt them. "Shout louder!" he said. "Surely he is a god! Perhaps he is deep in thought, or busy, or traveling. Maybe he is sleeping and must be awakened."

1 Kings 18:26–27

Baal never came! But when Elijah prayed, the God of Israel sent fire from heaven that consumed the sacrifice.

Other nations made idols from wood, stone, or metal to represent their gods. They would make temples to house the idols, pray to them, and offer them sacrifices. Many of these idols have been unearthed by archaeologists. They are on display in museums around the world.

The Bible pokes fun at the idols made to visualize these gods. For example, one of Israel's psalms in the Old Testament ridicules the powerlessness of the idols and the gods behind them:

> Our God is in heaven;
>   he does whatever pleases him.
> But their idols are silver and gold,
>   made by human hands.
> They have mouths, but cannot speak,
>   eyes, but cannot see.
> They have ears, but cannot hear,
>   noses, but cannot smell.
> They have hands, but cannot feel,
>   feet, but cannot walk,
>   nor can they utter a sound with their throats.
> Those who make them will be like them,
>   and so will all who trust in them.
>   Psalm 115:3–8

Are these gods real? Or are they the product of human superstition and fear? Do demons have anything to do with these gods and their idols?

The apostle Paul says yes, there are demonic powers behind the idols. He warns the Christians in the city of Corinth to stay far away from idolatry. If they belong to Jesus, they should not eat at the temple of an idol, where the food comes from an animal sacrificed to the idol.

Do I mean then that food sacrificed to an idol is anything, or that an idol is anything? No, but the sacrifices of pagans are offered to demons, not to God, and I do not want you to be participants with demons. You cannot drink the cup of the Lord [Jesus] and the cup of demons too; you cannot have a part in both the Lord's table and the table of demons.

1 Corinthians 10:19–21

Notice Paul teaches us that demons receive the sacrifices offered to gods and idols. These people are actually worshiping demons when they bow before an idol. That means there may be real, evil power behind the idols. The threat of demon attacks on idol worshipers seems to be a distinct possibility. Paul warns that followers of Christ should stay away from idols.

Surely we do not have idols today, do we? Maybe we do not have images of gods carved into wood or stone that we bow down to. But twenty-first-century idolatry may take the form of attention to created things that belongs only to the one God of heaven. Idolatry can be defined as our devotion to anything that captures our complete focus and loyalty. We look to it to give our lives meaning and excitement. We live for the idol.

Based on that understanding of idolatry, we have many candidates today in the sports world, movies, music, and other forms of entertainment. If someone's entire life is devastated and they suffer from depression when their sports team loses in the playoffs, it might qualify as idolatry. People and possessions can become idols, too, if they are more important to us than God.

The Bible does not speak to the issue, but might demons take advantage of our idols to gain a foothold in our lives?

32 Did demons mate with women long ago?

S atan and the demons intrigue us. Our curiosity is aroused trying to understand the evil spirits' existence. What is it like to
be a spirit-being that is thoroughly twisted by evil? What things
would a creature like that be able to do? We are drawn in by the
unknown abilities of demons. Some Bible passages in particular
raise questions about demons. One story in Genesis stands out.

Very early on in human history, even before Noah and the flood,
Genesis tells a mysterious story:

> When human beings began to increase in number on the earth
> and daughters were born to them, the sons of God saw that the
> daughters of humans were beautiful, and they married any of them
> they chose. Then the Lord said, "My Spirit will not contend with
> humans forever, for they are mortal; their days will be a hundred
> and twenty years."
>
> The Nephilim were on the earth in those days—and also after-
> ward—when the sons of God went to the daughters of humans and
> had children by them. They were the heroes of old, men of renown.
>
> Genesis 6:1–4

At first look, Genesis appears to teach that angelic beings, "the
sons of God," married human women and fathered a race of beings
called the Nephilim. The angelic-human union does not seem to
please God. He responds by limiting how long humans will live.
How do we understand what this story describes? Did demons
really mate with women long ago?

Such an understanding fits with ancient stories of angel-human
unions in other civilizations. In popular entertainment, movies
such as *Rosemary's Baby* and *Demon Seed* use the same plot. Is

the Genesis story really teaching that demons mated with human women?

Back to the Bible's account, this Genesis story is difficult to interpret correctly. The "sons of God" in the Old Testament refers to angels in several places. For example, in one passage, God refers to angels being present when the earth was created:

> On what were its footings set,
>   or who laid its cornerstone—
> while the morning stars sang together
>   and all the angels shouted for joy?
>   Job 38:6–7

Literally, the passage says that the "sons of God" shouted for joy. The translators identified these sons of God as "angels" in their choice of words.

The Genesis story says that these sons of God married the daughters of men, clearly referring to human women. They produced sons that are called the Nephilim, which means "fallen ones,"[1] or those who make others fall because they are "heroes" or "mighty men" (KJV).

Are these fallen angels, then, who mated with human women to produce the mighty but sinful men of old? Interpreters of the Genesis story do not agree. Some say that the sons of God and daughters of men are two different family lines that should not have intermarried. Other interpreters say that the sons of God were kings and mighty men long ago who sinned by marrying many wives—"any of [the women] they chose"—the beginning of harems.

If the sons of God are fallen angels, they must have joined themselves to these women in marriage, not merely having sexual relations with them, according to the Genesis story. There is no other mention of angels or demons doing such a thing in the Bible. In addition, how do spirit-beings marry humans, who are physical creatures? Do they take human form? Angels have the ability to appear as humans if they wish to do so. But no Bible passage ever indicates that angels remain in human form and marry human women. Is the apostle Peter teaching us about the Genesis story in this reference?

> God did not spare angels when they sinned, but sent them to hell, putting them in chains of darkness to be held for judgment. . . . [God] did not spare the ancient world when he brought the flood on its ungodly people, but protected Noah, a preacher of righteousness, and seven others.
>
> 2 Peter 2:4–5

This view says that the sin of the sons of God was demons taking human form to marry women, producing the powerful, evil Nephilim. The interpretation is possible, because it fits the context of the story in Genesis. Peter goes on in the next verse to speak of God's judgment during the time of Noah. In Genesis, the story of these sons of God is followed by the story of Noah.

A similar understanding teaches that the sons of God possessed the kings and mighty men of long ago, moving them to produce the Nephilim. We have seen from other Scripture passages that such a demonization is possible, as well.

Other than to satisfy our curiosity to understand the Bible, the Genesis account of the sons of God does not affect our lives directly. If they were demons marrying human women, no evidence from the Bible points to such a union taking place after this time long ago. The story does provide us with more evidence, however, that Satan and the demons are intent on harassing the human race, destroying us if they can. We all should take heed.

33 What is hell? Is it a real place? Where is it?

Hell is the ultimate nightmare. Nothing else compares. Hell's threat of suffering and torture is stamped on our world's mind and heart. We wish our enemies to go there in moments of anger. We are motivated to behave ourselves because of its horror. Hell can reduce the tenderhearted to tears. It is a formidable subject.

But is it real? What is hell? Are our fears justified? The Bible gives us a lot of information about hell. Jesus himself teaches about hell more than anyone else in the Bible. We have something to go on.

Hell goes by several names in the Bible. This place of suffering is also called Sheol, Hades, Gehenna, Tartarus, and the Lake of Fire.

The Old Testament uses two words for hell. One is *Sheol*. The Hebrews understood Sheol to be the place of the dead, where all people live when they die—rich and poor, good and evil.[1] It wasn't so much a place of suffering as a bland existence at rest or asleep. Job describes the afterlife as restful for those who have suffered on earth:

> There the wicked cease from turmoil,
> and there the weary are at rest.
> Captives also enjoy their ease;
> they no longer hear the slave driver's shout.
> The small and the great are there,
> and the slaves are freed from their owners.
> Job 3:17–19

From Greek mythology, Sheol's equivalent was Hades, the place of the dead ruled by the god Hades.[2] Sheol, or Hades, was the place of the dead, "the pit," or "the grave."

Another idea for the place of the dead developed in the Old Testament and up to the time of Jesus. The Jews used the term *Gehenna* for the place of the dead. But it was no quiet place of rest. Gehenna refers to a valley just outside Jerusalem that was used for child sacrifice to the Canaanite god Molech (2 Chronicles 28:3). After Judah's King Josiah destroyed Molech's altar there, the valley served as a dumping ground for garbage. To keep the stench down, fires burned continually in Gehenna.[3]

Jesus uses the imagery of perpetual fire and defilement embedded in the idea of Gehenna to describe the unending suffering for those who reject Him and come under God's judgment. His warnings are serious:

> And if your eye causes you to stumble, pluck it out. It is better for you to enter the kingdom of God with one eye than to have two eyes and be thrown into hell [*Gehenna*], where "the worms that eat them do not die, and the fire is not quenched."

> Mark 9:47–48

A burning garbage dump includes both fire and maggots, which Jesus uses to paint the picture of Gehenna. It is an awful image, meant to motivate us to avoid it at any cost.

Jesus tells us that this place of fire was made as the place of judgment for Satan and the demons (Matthew 25:41). The apostle Peter adds that the worst of the angels are in chains in *Tartarus* (2 Peter 2:4), the most terrible place of torment in hell according to Greek myth. The lost join them forever and ever.

Hell is not pictured as an idea or a state of mind, but a real place that people are doomed to inhabit. It has no equal on earth. We struggle to grasp the raw horror of judgment in hell. Separation from God, under His wrath, is more horrifying than anything we can imagine.

There is a way, just one way, to avoid hell. Thankfully, Jesus is all about bringing glory to God by rescuing us from judgment so that we can be with Him for all time:

95

For God so loved the world that he gave his one and only Son, that whoever believes in him shall not perish but have eternal life. For God did not send his Son into the world to condemn the world, but to save the world through him.

John 3:16–17

There are much better reasons to become a follower of Christ. But this remains a very good reason—avoid God's judgment and the misery of hell! Put your faith in Christ today.

34 Do Satan and the demons torment people in hell?

What do those in hell experience? Everyone seems to have their own idea. A popular fiction about hell today comes from those who say, "I want to go to hell. Heaven would be boring after a while. But I will be in hell with all my buddies, and we can party every night!" Unfortunately, such a view is misinformed. Hell is a terrible place. We should do all we can to avoid it. The Bible teaches that those in hell are separated from God forever, without hope, and miserable. Those who die apart from Jesus Christ are banished to hell with Satan and the demons.

Another view of hell is popular today, that hell is a place where demons torment the lost human souls there.[1] Does the Bible teach that demons torture humans cast into hell?

We read in the Bible that demons torture people in this life. Luke records a father speaking to Jesus about his son: "[The spirit] has often thrown him into fire or water to kill him" (Mark 9:22).

The Bible also reports demons tormenting a man to the point where he is in agony and tries to harm himself: "Night and day among the tombs and in the hills he would cry out and cut himself with stones" (Mark 5:5).

During the end times, before Jesus returns, the Bible records demonic creatures unleashed to bring intense suffering to the people on the earth:

> They were not allowed to kill [the people] but only to torture them for five months. And the agony they suffered was like that of the sting of a scorpion when it strikes.
>
> Revelation 9:5

Do demons continue to torment humans in the afterlife? The Bible makes no mention of it. The Bible portrays hell as a place where the wrath of God is unleashed against those humans whom God has judged. In one of the most horrifying passages in the Bible, the apostle John records an angel's declaration about what will happen to those who reject God and are banished to hell:

> They, too, will drink the wine of God's fury, which has been poured full strength into the cup of his wrath. They will be tormented with burning sulfur in the presence of the holy angels and of [Jesus Christ]. And the smoke of their torment will rise for ever and ever. There will be no rest day or night.
>
> Revelation 14:10–11

The passage teaches that humans in hell are tormented by God, not evil spirits. The time for demons to attack humans is over. They now fall under God's wrath themselves:

> And the devil, who deceived [the nations], was thrown into the lake of burning sulfur, where the beast and the false prophet had been thrown. They will be tormented day and night for ever and ever.
>
> Revelation 20:10

Hell troubles anyone with half a heart for others. Words fail to capture hell's ghastly reality. We can only imagine inadequately the existence of such a place.

The hope that shines through the clouds is that all of us humans can avoid this awful place. The Lord Jesus Christ promises life for those who believe in Him and become His followers: "Very truly I tell you, whoever hears my word and believes him who sent me has eternal life and will not be judged but has crossed over from death to life" (John 5:24).

Following Jesus not only saves us from the horrors of hell. We also come to know God and His love, to be enjoyed with Him for all eternity. If you are not yet a follower of Jesus Christ, what are you waiting for?

35 Do those in hell really burn forever?

Hell today is not what it used to be. The sober ways people used to think and talk about hell have been softened, or eliminated altogether. Expressions that once carried great weight find their way into our petty frustrations or anger. Someone cuts me off in traffic, and my response may be to wish eternal punishment for them.

Hell just doesn't sound that serious anymore. Why be afraid of life after death in hell?

Will those in hell really burn forever? What does the Bible say?

The Scriptures paint a clear picture. Hell is a place of endless suffering. The most common way hell is described is fire that never ends. At judgment, those who die without Christ are dispatched to the "lake of fire" (Revelation 20:14). The lake of fire is described in detail:

> They, too, will drink the wine of God's fury, which has been poured full strength into the cup of his wrath. They will be tormented with burning sulfur in the presence of the holy angels and of the Lamb. And the smoke of their torment will rise forever and ever.
>
> Revelation 14:10–11

Is the fire real? Will the lost actually suffer forever? Or are these figures of speech describing the horror of being separated from God's love? People through the centuries have challenged the teaching of hell's fire. Some groups claim that the endless fire of hell signals that God snuffs out of existence those who are judged. They die—body, soul, and spirit.[1] They do not suffer forever. This view has gained popularity in the last twenty-five years.[2]

Another centuries-old challenge to the biblical teaching of hell has resurfaced in recent years. This view says that no one will suffer forever in hell. Because God's love is infinite and eternal, all humans will have an unlimited number of chances through all time to believe in Jesus Christ after they die. Everyone in hell eventually comes to follow Christ.[3]

When these alternative views are evaluated against Scripture, they seem to struggle to interpret the key Bible passages fairly and accurately. Although it is a horrifying reality, the Bible teaches that all who die without becoming a follower of Christ will suffer under God's wrath forever. We cannot ignore or explain away the Bible's teaching in the matter without risking a grave error and putting people at risk through false assurances.

The Bible declares that a day will come when God judges the earth. All those who die without faith in Christ will face the endless wrath of God. The good news is that today is not that day! Today is the day of salvation. Come to Christ for the forgiveness of sin and you will be prepared for the day of judgment.

36 How can a kind, loving God send anyone to a place like hell?

A question circulates over and over. It has to do with two realities that do not seem to be compatible. One reality: God is our kind, loving, merciful creator. The other reality is hell, the place where God sends people to be punished eternally. How can both be true? It seems that either God is not, in fact, kind and merciful, or that hell cannot really exist or be all that bad.

Lots of people have denied God's existence because of the Bible's teaching on hell. We just don't seem to be able to accept what the Bible clearly says. It seems to violate any understanding we might have of God's love and mercy. Let's look more closely at what the Bible teaches.

Yes, thankfully, God is kind, loving, and merciful. The Bible declares it again and again. For example:

> The Lord is gracious and compassionate,
>   slow to anger and rich in love.
> The Lord is good to all;
>   he has compassion on all he has made.
>   Psalm 145:8–9

This description of God is repeated eight times in the Old Testament. Clearly, God wishes to be known as gracious, compassionate, patient, loving, and good. The New Testament echoes the same characteristics of God:

Whoever does not love does not know God, because God is love. This is how God showed his love among us: He sent his one and only Son into the world that we might live through him.

1 John 4:8–9

The Bible also informs us about God's judgment: "The wrath of God is being revealed from heaven against all the godlessness and wickedness of people, who suppress the truth by their wickedness" (Romans 1:18).

When we think about God, we must remember to include all of who God is, not just what suits us. In today's world, we tend to overdo God's love. Everyone wishes to make God out as kind, benevolent, and caring. (And He is all of those things!) Few of us, however, also want to think of God as judging people justly in His anger and wrath.

The Bible helps us understand God as a whole being. God makes himself known as loving and merciful, but He also reveals himself in the Bible as just. Jesus speaks about the judgment that God the Father and He will render someday, referring to himself as the "Son of Man":

And [the Father] has given him authority to judge because he is the Son of Man. Do not be amazed at this, for a time is coming when all who are in their graves will hear his voice and come out—those who have done what is good will rise to live, and those who have done what is evil will rise to be condemned.

John 5:27–29

God is just. He rewards good and punishes evil. God must judge sinful people who refuse to turn from their ways if He is to be perfectly just. He will right every wrong.

Compare God's love and justice to a neighborhood police officer. When he rescues my cat from a tree, gives me directions when I am lost, or gives me a ride home after my car breaks down, he is good, compassionate, and kind. But the same cop is strong, strict, and sometimes violent when he confronts criminals on the street.

In a similar way, God is kind and strict, loving and just, merciful and righteous.

We need to remember what the Bible says about all of us. Humans are sinful to the core, corrupted and rebellious against God. The apostle Paul declares this: "There is no one righteous, not even one; there is no one who understands; there is no one who seeks God" (Romans 3:10–11).

Do we really need the Bible to tell us about human sin? Just look around. The world groans under the effects of sin. Evil abounds in societies that we humans have created. And just one look into each of our hearts reveals the capacity for such horrible, evil things that it takes our breath away! The Bible is right. We all are sinners.

Because of human sin and rebellion against God, the problem isn't God sending people to hell. The problem is, why does He choose to save any of us *from* hell? If what Paul says is true, God would be perfectly just to cast all of us into hell: "For the wages of sin is death, but the gift of God is eternal life in Christ Jesus our Lord" (Romans 6:23).

Thank God that He is just and merciful. He gives us the gift of eternal life through Christ, something we cannot earn and something that He did not need to do. We do not deserve it. But it is ours through Jesus Christ.

37 What is spiritual warfare?

One of the constants of human existence is war. Soldiers kill each other in combat today just as people have for all of human history. War is ever present. It brings devastation, heartache, and loss.

The longest running war in history, however, is one seldom seen out in the open. It is a hidden battle, but millions of lives have been ruined as casualties of this war. This conflict is called spiritual warfare.

What is spiritual warfare? It is the ongoing battle between the forces of good and evil in the spiritual world. God and His angels wage war with Satan and his demonic host.

Because the human race does not live in the spiritual realm of existence, much about spiritual warfare remains a mystery to us. But we *do* know that the battle in the spiritual world carries over into our physical world, too. Because we have a spiritual nature, humans can be affected by this warfare. Demonic forces have the ability to enslave us to evil. They can win us over to their side, so that some humans actually end up fighting God. The Bible contains several stories about humans caught in the middle of the conflict as demonic powers sought to control them for their purposes. Today, many documented cases confirm that similar conflicts continued after Bible times.

Who will win the spiritual war? The Bible leaves no doubt! The Lord God Almighty will defeat Satan and his followers at the end of the age. All evil will be banished to hell when God judges the world. However, the final victory does not mean that every conflict today in the spiritual war will be won by God's forces. Satan and his wicked ways claim many victories in their assault on the human race.

How do we protect ourselves? Surrender to the enemy? No, the Bible urges us to fight the forces of evil. For example, the apostle Paul instructs us:

> Put on the full armor of God, so that you can take your stand against the devil's schemes. For our struggle is not against flesh and blood, but against the rulers, against the authorities, against the powers of this dark world and against the spiritual forces of evil in the heavenly realms.
>
> Ephesians 6:11–12

Notice several things from these verses. First of all, this is a dangerous war. We need armor from God to stand against Satan. Satan has devised plans to use against us, and it is a struggle. See also that the struggle is not against other humans but against spiritual rulers, authorities, powers, and forces of evil.

Without God protecting us, we cannot win the battle against the demonic armies of evil. That protection comes, first of all, by enlisting in God's forces. One of the really great results of becoming a follower of Jesus Christ is that we are issued God's armor to resist the devil. God equips us with His Word, the Bible. He gives us the truth of the gospel and salvation. And our trust in God's care will see us through. We find comfort, safety, and security as followers of Christ.

38 Who will win the spiritual war between God and Satan?

Few people are old enough to remember the first dark days of World War II. Germany swept across the continent of Europe, seeming to be unstoppable. By the end of summer 1940, one year into the war, Great Britain alone stood against the Nazi forces. Fear spread through the free world. People wondered if anything could stop Hitler's conquests.

As we noted in the previous chapter, there is an ongoing spiritual war between God and Satan. Even though we cannot observe the battles with our eyes, the spiritual war is real and dangerous. It sometimes seems that Satan has the upper hand and nothing can stop the evil in the world. It would be easy to be overwhelmed with fear just like those who lived during the early days of World

War II. Who will win? Will God prevail? Or will Satan and his dark host win the day?

Some believe that the battle will never be settled. God and Satan will fight one another throughout time. One side might win a few battles. But then the other side will claim victories, too. Back and forth, forever, good and evil wage war. This view is called dualism. Dualists believe that God and Satan are independent, equal forces in the world. Neither is able to defeat the other once and for all.[1]

The Bible's answer is much different. God wins the spiritual war that is raging today! He will defeat Satan and the dark powers finally and decisively, bringing all spiritual warfare to an end. Many biblical texts describe God's ultimate victory. For instance, Revelation 20:10 says, "And the devil, who deceived [the people], was thrown into the lake of burning sulfur, where the beast and the false prophet had been thrown. They will be tormented day and night for ever and ever."

Even the demons know that their defeat is coming. When Jesus confronted the evil spirits terrorizing two men, the demons appealed to Him: "'What do you want with us, Son of God?' they shouted. 'Have you come here to torture us before the appointed time?'" (Matthew 8:29).

These demons know that the "appointed time" of judgment is coming for them. They fear that Jesus will torment them now, before that time comes. They dread what they know will happen. Jesus will judge them and cast them into the lake of burning sulfur.

The apostle Paul also teaches us that after Satan is defeated, Jesus Christ will be declared Lord of all, even by the demons:

> Therefore God exalted [Jesus] to the highest place
> and gave him the name that is above every name,
> that at the name of Jesus every knee should bow,
> in heaven and on earth and under the earth,
> and every tongue acknowledge that Jesus Christ is Lord,
> to the glory of God the Father.
> Philippians 2:9–11

Even Satan and the demons must submit to Jesus. They still hate God and Jesus. But before they are banished to the lake of burning sulfur, they are forced to kneel before Jesus and admit that He is Lord.

Some of the greatest music ever penned celebrates God's victory over Satan. The "Hallelujah Chorus" from Handel's *Messiah* stands out among the rest:

> The kingdom of this world
> Is become the kingdom of our Lord,
> And of His Christ, and of His Christ;
> And He shall reign for ever and ever,
> For ever and ever, forever and ever,
> King of kings, and Lord of Lords,
> King of kings, and Lord of Lords, . . .[2]

After Satan's defeat, God will remake the earth with no sin or evil. God will be present with His people forever:

> And I heard a loud voice from the throne saying, "Look! God's dwelling place is now among the people, and he will dwell with them. They will be his people, and God himself will be with them and be their God. 'He will wipe every tear from their eyes. There will be no more death' or mourning or crying or pain, for the old order of things has passed away."
>
> Revelation 21:3–4

All of those people who have suffered, mourned, or cried in pain because of the evil in this world long for the day described in this passage. The spiritual battle continues today, claiming many casualties. But just as the Allies defeated Hitler in World War II, the glorious day when God banishes Satan and all the evil in this world is coming. We can count on it!

39 What is Satan's plan of attack on the human race?

We read in the Bible that Satan is out to destroy God's creation any way he can. He targets human beings in particular because we bear God's image. A real declaration of spiritual war has been called, with battles fought every day. Most wars, however, go beyond just one battle after the other. Opposing sides always have an overall strategic objective in mind.

For example, in the first Persian Gulf War in 1990, Saddam Hussein's overall objective was to conquer Kuwait in order to plunder their oil riches. He sought to elevate his nation's economic and political power in the entire region. His strategy was to invade Kuwait quickly, fortify his troops within the conquered nation, and resist any outside efforts to extract his forces.

Can we identify an overall satanic plan against us? What are Satan's priorities, and how does he work to accomplish them? We may not be able to discover Satan's plan, but we can put together some of the details from what the Bible tells us the devil hopes to do. At least four strategic priorities stand out.

First, the Bible is clear that one of Satan's highest priorities is to work diligently to keep non-Christians in the dark about Jesus Christ and the gospel message. In one of His stories, Jesus compares Satan's efforts against non-Christians to birds eating up a farmer's seeds before they can take root and grow:

> This is the meaning of the parable: The seed is the word of God. Those along the path are the ones who hear, and then the devil comes and takes away the word from their hearts, so that they may not believe and be saved.
>
> Luke 8:11–12

When Jesus called the apostle Paul to spread the gospel, He explained Paul's mission:

I will rescue you from your own people and from the Gentiles. I am sending you to them to open their eyes and turn them from darkness to light, and from the power of Satan to God, so that they may receive forgiveness of sins and a place among those who are sanctified by faith in me.

Acts 26:17–18

In one scene, the devil tried to keep Paul and his message of Jesus away from the non-Christians in the town of Thessalonica: "For we wanted to come to you—certainly I, Paul, did, again and again—but Satan blocked our way" (1 Thessalonians 2:18).

Satan hates it when someone becomes a follower of Jesus Christ. He will do all he can to keep people from hearing the message. He knows that if they hear the good news of Jesus, they might put their faith in Him and become followers of Christ. Paul teaches that hearing the gospel is the first step to being saved from our sin and becoming part of God's family:

"Everyone who calls on the name of the Lord [Jesus] will be saved." How, then, can they call on the one they have not believed in? And how can they believe in the one of whom they have not heard? And how can they hear without someone preaching to them?

Romans 10:13–14

A second priority in Satan's plans is to keep followers of Christ from maturing in their faith. He will hinder us every way he can. If we struggle with anger, for instance, Satan is ready to use it to neutralize us: "'In your anger do not sin': Do not let the sun go down while you are still angry, and do not give the devil a foothold" (Ephesians 4:26–27).

Married couples, too, are warned to avoid long periods without sexual intimacy with one another:

Do not deprive each other [sexually] except perhaps by mutual consent and for a time, so that you may devote yourselves to prayer. Then come together again so that Satan will not tempt you because of your lack of self-control.

1 Corinthians 7:5

Satan uses many tactics to derail our growth as followers of Jesus. If he cannot keep us from faith in Christ, he will try to keep us from growing closer to Jesus.

Third, Satan works to defeat the church. He strives to divide the members of Christ's body so that they are rendered powerless. For example, Paul encourages us to be patient with those in the church who oppose us:

And the Lord's servant must not be quarrelsome but must be kind to everyone, able to teach, not resentful. Opponents must be gently instructed, in the hope that God will grant them repentance leading them to a knowledge of the truth, and that they will come to their senses and escape from the trap of the devil, who has taken them captive to do his will.

2 Timothy 2:24–26

When Paul confronted false teachers in the church at Corinth, he made it clear that their teaching was from Satan, even though they tried to pass themselves off as Christian leaders:

For such people are false apostles, deceitful workers, masquerading as apostles of Christ. And no wonder, for Satan himself masquerades as an angel of light. It is not surprising, then, if his servants also masquerade as servants of righteousness. Their end will be what their actions deserve.

2 Corinthians 11:13–15

These false teachers brought division into the Corinthian church. It is one of Satan's top priorities, to divide Jesus Christ's church.

Finally, a fourth priority of Satan is to control the world's power and influence to spread his message of deceit. Paul describes the devil as "the god of this age" (2 Corinthians 4:4). Paul also links Satan to the world's powers. He reminds the Ephesian Christians of where they have come from:

> As for you, you were dead in your transgressions and sins, in which you used to live when you followed the ways of this world and of the ruler of the kingdom of the air, the spirit who is now at work in those who are disobedient.
>
> Ephesians 2:1–2

Satan uses the powers and attractions of this sinful world to his ends. It is a major way that Satan keeps people from faith in Christ. He keeps followers of Christ from growing closer to Jesus. He divides the church of Christ.

When we discover Satan's plans, we can stand against them more effectively, with the power of God Almighty working on our behalf. Martin Luther said it well almost five hundred years ago:

> For still our ancient foe doth seek to work us woe;
> His craft and power are great, and, armed with cruel hate,
> On earth is not his equal. . . .
>
> And though this world, with devils filled, should threaten
> to undo us,
> We will not fear, for God hath willed His truth to triumph
> through us:
> The Prince of Darkness grim, we tremble not for him;
> His rage we can endure, for lo, his doom is sure,
> One little word shall fell him.[1]

40 Do we have any power over Satan?

Action comic books make a fortune by pitting superheroes against the forces of evil. In recent years, many of the most popular movies are screen adaptations of these comic book champions: Batman, Spider-Man, Iron Man, Superman, Captain America, and the list goes on. These heroes appeal to us because they take on evil and defeat it. We enjoy triumphing over evil.

When we look at the might of Satan, we may feel the same urge. Do we have any power over the Prince of Darkness? Can we take on evil spirits and win? The apostle Paul speaks of victory over Satan: "The God of peace will soon crush Satan under your feet" (Romans 16:20).

Before we become overconfident, however, in our ultimate success against Satan, it is wise to bring in more of the Bible's teaching on the subject. Three passages in particular temper our enthusiasm to take on evil powers. The apostle Peter warns followers of Christ to be humble and cautious when encountering evil spirits. He speaks about some in the church who were confronting demons:

> Bold and arrogant, they are not afraid to heap abuse on celestial beings; yet even angels, although they are stronger and more powerful, do not heap abuse on such beings when bringing judgment on them from the Lord. But these people blaspheme in matters they do not understand. They are like unreasoning animals, creatures of instinct, born only to be caught and destroyed, and like animals they too will perish.
>
> 2 Peter 2:10–12

Peter acknowledges that these celestial beings are powerful. Even God's angels are careful in the way that they speak to them. By being bold and arrogant with evil spirits, these people are destroying themselves.

In his brief letter in the New Testament, Jude tells us that Michael, one of God's highest angels, knew the power of the adversary that he confronted:

> But even the archangel Michael, when he was disputing with the devil about the body of Moses, did not himself dare to condemn him for slander but said, "The Lord rebuke you!"
>
> Jude 1:9

We don't know all of the details surrounding this confrontation between Michael and Satan, but it is clear that Satan's powers demanded respect.

The Bible warns us not to think that we ourselves have any power over demons. The good news is that God Almighty has *all* power over these dark spirits. And Jesus confers on His followers God's authority to face demons. When Jesus sent out His followers to proclaim the good news of salvation, He equipped them with the authority that they needed to succeed:

> When Jesus had called the Twelve [apostles] together, he gave them power and authority to drive out all demons and to cure diseases, and he sent them out to proclaim the kingdom of God and to heal the sick.
>
> Luke 9:1–2

When they returned, Christ's followers reported to Jesus:

> [They] returned with joy and said, "Lord, even the demons submit to us in your name."
>
> He replied, "I saw Satan fall like lightning from heaven. I have given you authority to trample on snakes and scorpions and to

overcome all the power of the enemy; nothing will harm you. However, do not rejoice that the spirits submit to you, but rejoice that your names are written in heaven."

Luke 10:17–20

Notice that the demons submit to Christ's followers, but only in the name of Jesus. It is Jesus who has the power over evil spirits. Any authority we have is only as we identify with the Lord Jesus Christ and remain united with Him.

In addition, when the followers of Jesus cast out demons in His name, it is not just by saying His name that evil spirits flee. Jesus' name is not some magic incantation. Some people needed to learn this lesson the hard way in the book of Acts. When Paul was spreading the gospel in the town of Ephesus, he was given God's power to cast out demons. Luke records that seven non-Christian brothers in Ephesus sought to imitate Paul's actions:

> Some Jews who went around driving out evil spirits tried to invoke the name of the Lord Jesus over those who were demon-possessed. They would say, "In the name of the Jesus whom Paul preaches, I command you to come out." Seven sons of Sceva, a Jewish chief priest, were doing this. One day the evil spirit answered them, "Jesus I know, and Paul I know about, but who are you?" Then the man who had the evil spirit jumped on them and overpowered them all. He gave them such a beating that they ran out of the house naked and bleeding.

Acts 19:13–16

These men thought there was magical power over demons in simply using the names of Jesus and Paul. Their experience teaches us all. Jesus possesses all power over Satan and his host. We only have the authority to act against these dark powers as we remain dependent on Jesus to exert His power through us.

113

41 Does Satan rule over the world today?

Satan is a strong, cunning creature, dedicated to achieve his evil purposes. As Martin Luther put it, "His craft and power are great, and, armed with cruel hate, on earth is not his equal."[1] The devil also rules over the demonic host as their prince. How much further does that rule extend? What authority does Satan have? Does he rule over the world today?

The Bible affirms that Satan possesses significant authority to act against the human race. Jesus calls Satan the "prince of this world" (John 12:31). The apostle Paul describes him as the "ruler of the kingdom of the air" (Ephesians 2:2) and the "god of this age" (2 Corinthians 4:4). As a result, Satan commands all the other "spiritual forces of evil in the heavenly realms" (Ephesians 6:12).

God grants the devil authority over the world because of sin. Just like the devil, the human race is corrupted by sin. When we rebel against God, we join forces with the Prince of Darkness whether we choose to do so or not. We come under his power. Paul explains the evil work that Satan performs on all sinful humanity: "The god of this age has blinded the minds of unbelievers, so that they cannot see the light of the gospel that displays the glory of Christ, who is the image of God" (2 Corinthians 4:4).

We all come under the power of Satan, unable to do anything about it. Thankfully, God takes the initiative to save us from the devil. When Jesus called Paul to proclaim the gospel, He explained to Paul the result that would come from his efforts:

> I am sending you to them to open their eyes and turn them from darkness to light, and from the power of Satan to God, so that they

may receive forgiveness of sins and a place among those who are sanctified by faith in me.

Acts 26:17–18

The word *power* in these verses also means "authority" or "dominion."[2] God rescues us from Satan's authority over us. Satan rules over the sinful human race, but his grip on us is broken by the ruler over all, the Lord Jesus Christ.

42 What is the occult? Does Satan have anything to do with the occult?

E very so often, the occult pops up in the news. Sometimes associated with popular entertainment, at times the occult also plays a role in criminal investigations. Murder, theft, or other violent acts are tied to occult influences. What is behind all of this? What is the occult? Does Satan have anything to do with it?

The word *occult* means hidden or concealed. It usually refers to secret or hidden activities in the paranormal/supernatural realm (powers and experiences that go beyond the five senses). Some of the most well-known occult practices are magic, spiritism, and divination.

Magic

Magic is extremely naturalistic.[1] It divides into many branches, all holding their unique views. On the whole, magic claims to manipulate natural and supernatural forces through the use of spells, incantations, and potions (chemical formulas). Some forms of magic acknowledge spirits working through natural materials.[2]

Magic appears early in the Bible. Five hundred years before Christ, "magicians, enchanters, sorcerers and astrologers" (Daniel 2:2) served King Nebuchadnezzar in Babylon. The Christmas story also includes those who practiced magic: "After Jesus was born in Bethlehem in Judea, during the time of King Herod, Magi from the east came to Jerusalem" (Matthew 2:1).

Among those who practice magic, there are starkly different views of Satan's involvement in their craft. Black magic often declares its allegiance to Satan,[3] while white magic rejects any link to the devil.[4]

Spiritism

The occult practice of spiritism, or necromancy, teaches that humans survive death as spirits. Mediums, or channels (people who say that they possess a special psychic gift), claim to contact the dead through séances and other rituals.

The Bible does not address spiritism in any detail. But it does repeatedly prohibit the practice (Leviticus 19:31; 20:27; Isaiah 8:19; 2 Kings 21:6). There is enough said about spiritism in the Bible that it should not be ignored. It is an occult practice that may have satanic ties.

Divination

Divination is any attempt to discover the future. It is associated with other parts of the occult. For example, mediums who try to contact the dead often do so to learn the future. Some of the most widely practiced forms of divination are astrology, tarot cards, palm reading, and the use of divining rods. The Bible warns against divination (Leviticus 19:26; 1 Samuel 15:23).

഼

The Bible does not speak to occult practices often. But Moses denounced all occult activities in his farewell message to Israel before they entered their Promised Land:

When you enter the land the Lord your God is giving you, do not learn to imitate the detestable ways of the nations there. Let no one be found among you who sacrifices their son or daughter in the fire, who practices divination or sorcery, interprets omens, engages in witchcraft, or casts spells, or who is a medium or spiritist or who consults the dead. Anyone who does these things is detestable to the Lord; because of these same detestable practices the Lord your God will drive out those nations before you. You must be blameless before the Lord your God.

Deuteronomy 18:9–13

Occult practices are hateful to God because His people are trusting in powers other than God for their lives and fortunes. We are to look to God for all our needs and trust Him with our future.

In addition, the occult is repugnant to God because of its ties to Satan in many of its practices. God warns us to stay clear of the occult. Demons are associated with many occult activities. We run the risk of welcoming demonic powers into our lives by dabbling in the occult.

43 Is it wrong to watch movies or read books about the occult?

Some of the most popular films of the last few years include strong themes of magic, witches, and demons. Hollywood continues to produce these films because they are consistent money-makers. Some of the most popular fiction today also delves into the occult and superstition—the Harry Potter books, the *Twilight* book series, and even *The Lord of the Rings*.

Is it wrong to watch movies or read books about the occult? You can hardly avoid it! There may not be an easy yes or no answer. But the Bible does help us to discern our best course of action.

On the one hand, it may be the wisest thing for us to avoid movies, television, and books that include occult practices like magic, fortune-telling, and spiritism. These entertainment media influence us at a deeply personal level, more than we may realize or desire. Our minds and hearts are very susceptible to outside influences.

Human beings are more vulnerable than we may wish to admit. Outside forces have the ability to shape our thinking, manipulate our behavior, and play with our emotions. For example, we cry sincere tears of grief when Bambi's mother is killed. We are stirred to outrage over human exploitation of the natural resources of a fictitious planet populated by blue creatures. And our hearts are warmed by the romance between two robots who fall for each other on a dead earth covered with garbage. The stories are pure fiction, but our thoughts and feelings are very real.

Television commercials exploit human vulnerability every day. Many of us can still hum the jingles created for McDonald's commercials decades ago. Ideas get into our minds and hearts without our permission. They affect the way we make sense of the world around us and our place in it. It is a great mistake to underestimate the power of suggestion or to overestimate our ability to resist these influences.

The media's portrayal of Satan, demons, and occult practices is often wrong, based on superstition and folklore. Nevertheless, those ideas seep into our thinking. We struggle to discern truth from fiction. What results can be either an unhealthy, misinformed fear of Satan and the occult, or a dangerous overconfidence about facing evil forces that have been tamed to become nothing more than benign sources of entertainment.

What do we allow into our minds and hearts? What is shaping our thinking—the truth about Satan and the occult, based on the Bible and sober study, or folklore drummed into our hearts by the entertainment industry?

For those who follow Christ, the Bible gives guidance about what we let into our minds.

> Do not be anxious about anything, but in every situation, by prayer and petition, with thanksgiving, present your requests to God. And the peace of God, which transcends all understanding, will guard your hearts and your minds in Christ Jesus. Finally, brothers and sisters, whatever is true, whatever is noble, whatever is right, whatever is pure, whatever is lovely, whatever is admirable—if anything is excellent or praiseworthy—think about such things.
>
> Philippians 4:6–8

The apostle Paul instructs us to think about true, noble, right, pure, lovely, and admirable things. And those efforts are connected with God guarding our hearts and minds.

Paul repeats the theme in another of his letters:

> Since, then, you have been raised with Christ, set your hearts on things above, where Christ is, seated at the right hand of God. Set your minds on things above, not on earthly things.
>
> Colossians 3:1–2

Why do we read the books or watch the films containing satanic or occult content? If it is just for the entertainment, we may wish to consider other, less dangerous ways to amuse ourselves.

Yet, on the other hand, we need to recognize our freedom in Christ to live for Him in ways not explicitly commanded in the Bible. The Bible does not address these forms of entertainment directly, so we must be cautious about forbidding activities that the Bible does not prohibit. Paul again gives us sound teaching. He reminds us that followers of Christ are God's servants. We, therefore, answer to God for our entertainment choices:

> Who are you to judge someone else's servant? To their own master, servants stand or fall. And they will stand, for the Lord is able to make them stand. . . . You, then, why do you judge your brother

119

or sister? Or why do you treat them with contempt? For we will all stand before God's judgment seat.

Romans 14:4, 10

Followers of Jesus seek to please Him with everything they do, including their choices of entertainment. Our passion to love our Savior is far more important to us than any pleasure that we might receive from leisure activities. We will give account to God someday for those choices.

What is the answer to our question, then? Should we watch movies or read books that contain satanic or occult practices? The Bible's guidance is that we are free to take part in these forms of entertainment, but we should exercise great caution and wisdom about what we allow into our minds and hearts. We may receive much more than we asked for! And our greatest desire should be to please Jesus Christ with everything that we do.

44 Are there really people who worship Satan?

Few words evoke as strong a response as *Satanist*. Satanism dates back centuries, and people respond to it with curiosity, fear, and even fascination. Several high-profile crimes in the U.S. in the last forty years are connected with Satanism. Recently, Miranda Barbour, the alleged Craigslist Killer, said that there are Satanist connections to the more than twenty-two murders she claims to have committed.[1]

Some claim Satanists are part of almost every community in America, secretly practicing their rituals. Satanists who are willing to identify themselves maintain several prominent websites.

Their claims range widely. One of the most visible Satanists of the twentieth century was Howard LaVey. He founded the Church of Satan and changed his name to Anton LaVey.

The Church of Satan rejects God, advocating that humans reach their own potential through their self-will. LaVey advocated sensual indulgence, self-interest, and always satisfying one's desires and urges.[2]

LaVey played up his sinister image, wearing a long, black high-necked cloak and sporting a goatee and shaved head. The Church of Satan continued to operate after LaVey's death in 1997.

Satanists appear in other regions of the world, too. One group who dates back centuries is the Yezidi devil worshipers in Iraq.[3] A closed society suspicious of outsiders, the Yezidi people have been heavily persecuted all through their existence. They still maintain a form of devil worship today.

Several high-profile musical groups in the last fifty years have identified themselves with Satan or Satanists. The groups' names alone generate a good deal of anxiety in parents: Black Sabbath, Mayhem, and dozens of other bands from around the world.

Are these groups truly committed to worshiping Satan? It is a fair question, but one that is difficult to answer. The image they project clearly declares allegiance to Satan. But some of the image may be more for the effect of notoriety and profit generated. Nothing else provokes a response like claiming to be a Satanist!

Satanism generates a lot of interest for its promotion of self, indulgence, and rebellion against authority and power. Several satanic sources reject the image of Satan taught by the Bible. They exchange the biblical description of Satan for a more benign creature or make Satan a symbol for their own self-centered moral convictions.

Does Satan crave human worship? He is portrayed as seeking the worship of Christ, as recorded in the gospel of Matthew: "Again, the devil took [Jesus] to a very high mountain and showed him all the kingdoms of the world and their splendor. 'All this I will give you,' he said, 'if you will bow down and worship me'" (Matthew 4:8–9).

It follows that Satan would bask in worship from any and all humans, too. Even if his human followers are not entirely serious about their devotion to Satan, it would seem reasonable that any form of Satan worship is a dangerous activity. Perhaps the draw to Satan betrays a fundamental human flaw, as well. We are drawn to the father of rebellion and evil because we, too, have a smaller version of the same rebellion within us.

We are challenged to turn from Satan and to forsake our rebellion against God. We are called to put our trust in Jesus Christ to do two wonderful things for us: (1) pay for all our sin and rebellion through His death and (2) provide eternal joy, love, peace, and fulfillment. The apostle Paul explains God's wonderful actions for us:

> You see, at just the right time, when we were still powerless, Christ died for the ungodly. Very rarely will anyone die for a righteous person, though for a good person someone might possibly dare to die. But God demonstrates his own love for us in this: While we were still sinners, Christ died for us. Since we have now been justified by his blood, how much more shall we be saved from God's wrath through him! For if, while we were God's enemies, we were reconciled to him through the death of his Son, how much more, having been reconciled, shall we be saved through his life!
>
> Romans 5:6–10

We may never understand people worshiping Satan. God offers us, through the Lord Jesus Christ, something worth our worship.

45 Is it possible to show too much respect for Satan?

Satan is a strong, evil, crafty foe of the human race. We learn in the Bible, and through watching him in action, that the devil is able to bring incredible suffering into the world. We make a grave error by ignoring him or minimizing the threat that he poses to us. Is it possible, however, to go too far in the other direction? Can we err by showing too much respect to Satan? Can we give him too much attention?

The Bible always shows great respect for the devil's evil ways. The focus of the Bible, though, is God himself and the Lord Jesus Christ. God reveals himself in the Scriptures. His primary goal is that we come to know Him and to love Him. Any attention the Bible pays to Satan takes a distant second place to this premier purpose.

The number one priority for all human beings is to come to know God through His Son, the Lord Jesus Christ. God's plans for all of us begin with Christ bringing us peace with God through His sacrifice. The apostle Paul could not be clearer: "Here is a trustworthy saying that deserves full acceptance: Christ Jesus came into the world to save sinners—of whom I am the worst" (1 Timothy 1:15).

Then, when we become followers of Jesus Christ, we seek to grow closer to Him, first of all. Paul is our example:

> But whatever were gains to me I now consider loss for the sake of Christ. What is more, I consider everything a loss because of the surpassing worth of knowing Christ Jesus my Lord, for whose sake I have lost all things. I consider them garbage, that I may gain Christ.
>
> Philippians 3:7–8

As followers of Christ, Satan is not our focus. Our greatest attention should be given to Christ and pleasing Him.

46 Is fortune-telling (divination) demonic?

Do you know what the future holds for you? Will you gain great wealth? Will you find love? Or are pain and tragedy in your coming days? Questions like these penetrate almost all levels of popular culture. We long to know our futures. It's fun to wonder whether fortune cookies, the stars, or prophets can tell us what is in store for us.

Curiosity about the future makes many plot lines in popular entertainment, too. Stories either look ahead in life or go back into the past for another chance. In Charles Dickens's classic *A Christmas Carol*, Ebenezer Scrooge sees the horror of his future and repents. He is a changed man! And we are affected deeply ourselves. Just the chance to see our futures captivates our imaginations.

Many people profit from human curiosity about the future. Fortune-tellers offer us what is to come. Claiming special insight, contact with supernatural powers, or other special gifts, fortune-tellers are always popular.

The technical word for fortune-telling is *divination*. Divination is any type of occult attempt to forecast the future, to learn secrets, or to interpret omens or signs. Divination may take several paths, such as palm reading (chiromancy), reading the stars and horoscopes (astrology), interpreting tarot cards (cartomancy), prophets, and games such as a Ouija board.

Most of these activities appear harmless enough, but is that all there is to it? Are demonic powers behind any of these attempts to discover what tomorrow holds?

The Bible acknowledges that divination dates back thousands of years. Its connection to demonic powers surfaces in the New Testament. Luke writes in the book of Acts about the apostle Paul's confrontation with divination in the town of Philippi in Macedonia. Clearly, a demonic spirit was behind what was going on.

> Once when we were going to the place of prayer, we were met by a female slave who had [an evil] spirit by which she predicted the future. She earned a great deal of money for her owners by fortune-telling.
>
> Acts 16:16

Literally, Luke says that the girl had a "spirit of Python,"[1] referring to a snake god in Greek mythology that was able to produce oracles predicting the future.[2] This demonic spirit had linked itself to ancient mythology about the gods. But Paul, in the power of Jesus Christ, cast the spirit out of the girl, landing him in jail for his troubles.

Does this mean that demons have the ability to predict the future? Not necessarily. No biblical teaching shows demons possessing knowledge of the future in any specific kind of way. Certainly they have the ability to masquerade as having knowledge of what is to come, but the Bible teaches that only God has such foresight.

Those who follow Christ should be cautious to engage in any form of fortune-telling, despite its popularity. We have a God who promises to tend to our every need. When it comes to the future, Jesus' words comfort us:

> Therefore I tell you, do not worry about your life, what you will eat or drink; or about your body, what you will wear. Is not life more than food, and the body more than clothes? Look at the birds of the air; they do not sow or reap or store away in barns, and yet your

heavenly Father feeds them. Are you not much more valuable than they? Can any one of you by worrying add a single hour to your life?

Matthew 6:25–27

What *is* important? Jesus makes it crystal clear for us:

But seek first [God's] kingdom and his righteousness, and all these things will be given to you as well. Therefore do not worry about tomorrow, for tomorrow will worry about itself. Each day has enough trouble of its own.

Matthew 6:33–34

Why seek knowledge of the future from occult sources that may have ties with demonic powers? We do much better to entrust ourselves into the hands of an all-knowing, loving God through the Lord Jesus Christ.

47 Are witches real?

It seems as though witches are everywhere! Little girls soliciting candy on Halloween appear dressed in black, adorned with tall, pointy hats and fake warts on their faces. Bumper stickers on cars declare the occupants as advocates of Wicca.

Popular entertainment draws many of us to stories about witches as well. Television viewers a generation ago remember Samantha the witch. Young people today love the books and movies about child witches in England attending a prep school for witchcraft. And who can forget the scary, green-faced Wicked Witch of the West in Oz?

Where did all of this come from? Are witches real? What exactly is a witch? Some investigation reveals that many people claim to know all about witches, but they do not agree with one another about much of it. A brief survey of dictionary definitions of *witch* shows that even dictionaries cannot agree on what a witch is. The most basic idea appears to be that witches are people who cast spells or practice magic.[1] As such, witches have been around for a long time. In several biblical passages, people are labeled as those who practice magic—soothsayers, enchanters, sorcerers, or diviners.[2] Witches surfaced through the later Middle Ages in Europe, extending into colonial American experience.

Today many groups claim to be witches. One of the largest uses the word *Wicca* to identify itself. Wicca is extremely diverse and decentralized in its beliefs and practices. Many Wiccans combine occult, neo-pagan, and earth-centered beliefs.[3]

Do witches really have powers that they exercise through magic? On the one hand, most of these practices remain shrouded in rumor, secret rituals, and hidden activities. Conclusive proof of magical practices remains elusive. In addition, much of what passes as magic today is, in fact, illusion. The greatest magicians are illusionists, giving the appearance of performing powerful actions, but really using sleight of hand, distraction, and quick movements to appear to perform magic.

Nevertheless, the Bible records sorcerers with real supernatural powers at their disposal. For example, in the book of Exodus, Moses displays God's power to the king of Egypt by turning his brother Aaron's walking staff into a serpent. Note Pharaoh's response:

> Pharaoh then summoned wise men and sorcerers, and the Egyptian magicians also did the same things by their secret arts: Each one threw down his staff and it became a snake. But Aaron's staff swallowed up their staffs.
>
> Exodus 7:11–12

Exodus does not report this scene as an illusion. The magicians of Egypt appeared to possess real powers. But where did the power come from? Do witches worship Satan? Does he give witches supernatural powers? Historically, much of the fear of witches was caused by the suspected link of witches to Satan. The Salem witch trials in the late 1600s were largely driven by fear of witches sold into Satan's service.[4]

When the Bible portrays the events surrounding the return of Jesus Christ in the book of Revelation, it pictures an evil, Satan-empowered beast performing similar feats of great power:

> Then I saw a second beast, coming out of the earth. It had two horns like a lamb, but it spoke like a dragon. It exercised all the authority of the first beast on its behalf, and made the earth and its inhabitants worship the first beast, whose fatal wound had been healed. And it performed great signs, even causing fire to come down from heaven to the earth in full view of the people. Because of the signs it was given power to perform on behalf of the first beast, it deceived the inhabitants of the earth. It ordered them to set up an image in honor of the beast who was wounded by the sword and yet lived. The second beast was given power to give breath to the image of the first beast, so that the image could speak and cause all who refused to worship the image to be killed.
>
> Revelation 13:11–15

Wiccans in particular disavow any connection to Satan. They consider Satan to be a Christian creation. However strong their rejection of Satan, it still remains possible that those who practice witchcraft are unknowingly linked with Satan. He is more than ready to deceive these witches into thinking that they are just tapping natural powers as they come under his control.

The Bible calls all followers of Christ to distance themselves from witches and witchcraft, along with other occult practices. We wish to find our strength and hope in God, not practices associated with witches.

48 Is Satan behind Halloween?

H alloween is one of the top five secular holidays in America. Its popularity seems to be growing steadily. It has become a profitable enterprise. Halloween activities range widely. Both children and adults jump right in with costumes, home decorations, and all kinds of treats. Where did Halloween come from? Is Satan behind it all?

Halloween combines several traditions that date back over a thousand years in Europe. The name comes from a contraction of All Hallow's Eve. It marked the evening before the observance of All Hallow's Day, a Christian holiday commemorating saints and martyrs. It is now called All Saints Day and is celebrated November 1. This holy, or *hallowed,* day was preceded by several ritual practices the night before, October 31.[1]

October 31 to November 2 also marked a Celtic pagan celebration of the fall harvest. Called *Samhain* (pronounced sow'-een), or "summer's end," it was believed this was a time when the natural and supernatural worlds came close together. Spirits and ghosts would roam the earth.[2]

There is some discussion about whether the Roman Catholic Church intentionally made All Saints Day coincide with Samhain in an effort to Christianize the pagan festival. Historians remain divided on the subject.

A third tradition recognized on October 31 is Reformation Day. It commemorates Martin Luther posting his ninety-five theses on the Wittenberg church door in 1517, widely seen as the start of the Protestant Reformation.[3]

What we observe for Halloween today blends features from at least two of these traditions. Is Satan behind Halloween? On the one hand, some Halloween activities have clear ties to the occult and demonic forces. People dress as demons, witches, vampires, and ghosts. Séances, magical games, and other occult rituals are mimicked.

On the other hand, many features of Halloween seem benign. Kids dress up as comic-book heroes, princesses, and pirates. They enjoy going door to door for candy treats.

As a result, American families, including those who are followers of Jesus Christ, vary greatly in their attitudes about Halloween and participation in the event.

The Bible takes a very strong stand against any association with the occult or evil spirits. Remember God's warning to His people Israel:

> When you enter the land the Lord your God is giving you, do not learn to imitate the detestable ways of the nations there. Let no one be found among you who sacrifices their son or daughter in the fire, who practices divination or sorcery, interprets omens, engages in witchcraft, or casts spells, or who is a medium or spiritist or who consults the dead. Anyone who does these things is detestable to the Lord; because of these same detestable practices the Lord your God will drive out those nations before you. You must be blameless before the Lord your God.
>
> Deuteronomy 18:9–13

Therefore, any participation in Halloween should be with a great deal of caution. In particular, keeping a good distance from the more sinister, demonic parts of the holiday appears to be the best course. We should be very careful to stay away from any activity that may open us to satanic influence, regardless of how innocent it may appear on the surface.

49 Is a séance demonic? Should we try to contact the dead?

The afterlife seems to be an irresistible lure for those of us on this side of the barrier of death. We long to know if there really is life after death. We dearly miss our dead loved ones, desiring at times to be able to speak to them again. And we wonder whether what our churches tell us about heaven and hell is all true.

Churches aren't the only ones speaking about the afterlife. A popular branch of the occult, spiritism, claims to be able to cross the divide into the spiritual domain of God and angels, reaching those who have died. In the last few decades, the New Age movement has tapped into these interests. Popularized by actress Shirley MacLaine, the New Age movement teaches that, through a medium or channeler, we can communicate with the spirits of those who have died.[1]

Outside of the New Age movement, many other people claim to be mediums. A quick survey of the Internet uncovers thousands of websites devoted to contacting the dead. A common claim of spiritists is to be able to communicate with the spirits of dead humans or with other nature spirits or angels through a medium or psychic reader. They use séances, trances, meditation, and telepathy to reach the spirits.[2] Another name for this type of activity is necromancy.

Usually spiritism is connected to divination, attempting to learn the future or other secrets. Presumably, the dead have access to knowledge about these things that we in this life cannot know.

Is there anything to spiritism? Can we really contact people who have died? The Bible gives us some clues. First, the Scriptures teach us that we do survive death. The apostle Paul anticipates what happens to the follower of Christ at death:

Therefore we are always confident and know that as long as we are at home in the body we are away from the Lord. For we live by faith, not by sight. We are confident, I say, and would prefer to be away from the body and at home with the Lord.

2 Corinthians 5:6–8

Paul clarifies for us that to live in this life, to be "at home in the body," means that we are not in heaven with the Lord Jesus Christ. He looks forward to death and being "away from the body and at home with the Lord." Jesus himself promised life after death in his conversation with a woman whose brother had just died: "I am the resurrection and the life. The one who believes in me will live, even though they die; and whoever lives by believing in me will never die" (John 11:25–26).

Can mediums communicate with those who have died? The Bible gives only a small bit of evidence that humans can access deceased humans through spiritism. And it is not conclusive evidence. For example, King Saul sought to speak to Samuel the prophet after Samuel had died. Saul solicited a medium to call up Samuel's spirit:

The king said to her, "Don't be afraid. What do you see?"

The woman said, "I see a ghostly figure coming up out of the earth."

"What does he look like?" he asked.

"An old man wearing a robe is coming up," she said.

Then Saul knew it was Samuel, and he bowed down and prostrated himself with his face to the ground.

Samuel said to Saul, "Why have you disturbed me by bringing me up?"

1 Samuel 28:13–15

We cannot be sure that Samuel's spirit actually appeared to Saul. It may have been a demonic impersonation of Samuel intending to deceive Saul. We do not have enough evidence from the Bible to confirm occult access to the spirit world. Nor can we be sure that demonic activity is behind necromancy. The Bible strongly warns people to stay away from such practices, especially those who follow Jesus Christ. We should not seek to learn secrets or what the future holds through these occultic means. God will let us know all we need to know about the future. Listen to Isaiah the prophet's rebuke when Israel sought out mediums: "When someone tells you to consult mediums and spiritists, who whisper and mutter, should not a people inquire of their God? Why consult the dead on behalf of the living?" (Isaiah 8:19).

It seems unwise and dangerous to seek knowledge through spiritists because evil spirits have the ability to deceive us when we enter into their domain and ignore the almighty God who promises His protection and guidance.

50 After all this, what do I need to know about Satan and demons?

E xamining Satan and the demons covers a lot of ground. What is most important to take away from our study? Three points stand out. The first is about Satan. He and the demons are real. The Bible describes them as evil spirit-beings who sinned against God long ago. They now dedicate themselves to destroying God's creation, with the human race dead center in their sights. Satan has a plan, he uses many tactics to accomplish it, and his devotion to his plan is unwavering. Satan works to keep non-Christians far away from God. He labors to divide and to discourage followers of Jesus Christ. And he controls the world powers around us.

The second point that stands out from our study is about God. The Lord God Almighty rules over everything, both the physical universe and the domain of spirit-beings. God loves what He has created. He is faithful to protect and preserve His handiwork. Through Jesus Christ, God pours out His love on the human race. Satan must submit to God's will. Finally, at the end of the age, God will banish Satan and all the demons to an eternity separate from Him.

The third point is about us. On its own, the human race is defenseless against Satan. We are not strong enough to resist him. We cannot match his intelligence or cleverness. Our only hope is to seek God's protection by becoming followers of Jesus Christ. When we receive forgiveness for our sins through the death of Jesus, we come to know and to love God. More than anything, we desire to please Him with our lives. And we seek to spread the word about Christ to everyone we know.

If you are not yet a follower of Jesus Christ, there is no better time than right now to put your trust in Him for the forgiveness of sin, peace with God, and protection against Satan. When we belong to God, Satan cannot reach us for evil. Even when we suffer, God uses it to help us become stronger and grow closer to Him.

If you do follow Christ, seek to know Him better every day. Commit your whole life to Him. And find peace and protection from Satan in God's loving care.

J

May God grant you life in Jesus Christ.

May He protect you from Satan and his host all the days of your life.

And may God draw us close to himself in love and kindness. Amen!

Notes

3. What does Satan look like?

1. "Satan," *Joy of Satan*, www.angelfire.com/empire/serpentis666/Satan.html.

4. How does Satan act against humans?

1. *Strong's Concordance*, #2616, *katadunasteuo*, http://biblehub.com/greek/2616.htm.

2. *Strong's Concordance*, #1139, *daimonizomai*, http://biblehub.com/greek/1139.htm.

7. What is demon possession?

1. *The Exorcist* (film), *Wikipedia*, http://en.wikipedia.org/wiki/The_Exorcist_%28film%29.

2. *Strong's Concordance*, #1139, *daimonizomai*, http://biblehub.com/greek/1139.htm.

8. What is exorcism?

1. Thayer and Smith, "Greek Lexicon entry for *exorkizo*," *The NAS New Testament Greek Lexicon*, 1999, www.biblestudytools.com/lexicons/greek/nas/exorkizo.html#Legend.

2. "Exorcism," *Wikipedia*, http://en.wikipedia.org/wiki/Exorcism.

3. "Exorcism in Christianity," *Wikipedia*, http://en.wikipedia.org/wiki/Exorcism_in_Christianity.

9. Is demon possession the same thing as mental illness?

1. "Exorcism—Scientific View," *Wikipedia*, http://en.wikipedia.org/wiki/Exorcism.

2. Chris Cook, "Demon Possession and Mental Illness," *Nucleus*, Autumn 1997, 13–17, www.cmf.org.uk/publications/content.asp?context=article&id=619.

12. How can I become a follower of Jesus?

1. *Strong's Concordance*, #3101, *mathétés*, http://biblehub.com/greek/3101.htm.

14. Was Satan created by God? How did Satan become evil?

1. Brown, Driver, Briggs and Gesenius, "Hebrew Lexicon entry for *heylel*," *The NAS Old Testament Hebrew Lexicon*, www.biblestudytools.com/lexicons /hebrew/nas/heylel.html.

2. The word *Lucifer* comes from the Latin Vulgate's translation of the Hebrew word *heylel*. It does not appear to be a proper noun but a Latin word for "morning star." See Daniel B. Wallace, "Is Lucifer the Devil in Isaiah 14:12?" *Bible.org*, March 22, 2010, https://bible.org/article/lucifer-devil-isaiah-1412-kjv -argument-against-modern-translations.

15. Is Satan responsible for every bad thing that happens, like war, famine, earthquakes, etc.?

1. Job's servant assumed that the fire was from God because it came from the sky. But we are informed that it was Satan that sent the fire from the sky to kill these servants and sheep.

16. If Jesus defeated Satan on the cross, why is Satan still active in the world today?

1. Jethro Mullen, Yoko Wakatsuki, and Chandrika Narayan, "Hiroo Onoda, Japanese soldier who long refused to surrender, dies at 91," *CNN News*, January 17, 2014, www.cnn.com/2014/01/17/world/asia/japan-philippines-ww2-soldier-dies.

17. Would God ever forgive Satan?

1. Will L. Thompson, "Softly and Tenderly Jesus Is Calling," 1880, www .cyberhymnal.org/htm/s/o/softlyat.htm.

20. How do I know if Satan is really attacking me or not?

1. Joseph M. Scriven, "What a Friend We Have in Jesus," 1855, http://library .timelesstruths.org/music/What_a_Friend_We_Have_in_Jesus.

22. Do demons inhabit specific places?

1. "Poll: One-Third of Americans Believe in Ghosts, UFOs," *Fox News*, October 25, 2007, www.foxnews.com/story/2007/10/25/poll-one-third-americans-believe-in-ghosts-ufos. "Most Americans Believe in Ghosts," *WND News*, February 7, 2003, www.wnd.com/2003/02/17494.

2. Popularized by C. Peter Wagner, ed., *Territorial Spirits: Insights Into Strategic Level Spiritual Warfare & Intercession* (Ventura, CA: Gospel Light, 1991).

3. John Dawson, *Taking Our Cities for God* (Lake Mary, FL: Charisma, 1989, 2001).

4. "What Is Spiritual Mapping?" *Australian Prayer Network*, http://ausprayer net.org.au/teaching/spiritual_mapping.php.

23. Should I worry about demons attacking me?

1. Patrick Zukeran, "The World of Animism," *Bible.org*, October 1, 2010, https://bible.org/article/world-animism.

24. Do demons have specific names that describe their roles, like a demon of lust, greed, lying, etc.?

1. Frank E. Peretti, *This Present Darkness* (Wheaton, IL: Crossway Books, 1986).

2. "Legion," *Encyclopaedia Britannica*, www.britannica.com/EBchecked/topic/335026/legion.

28. Just how many demons are there?

1. "Legion," *Encyclopaedia Britannica*, www.britannica.com/EBchecked/topic/335026/legion.

32. Did demons mate with women long ago?

1. Bodie Hodge, "Who Were the Nephilim?" *Answers in Genesis*, July 9, 2008, www.answersingenesis.org/articles/aid/v2/n1/who-were-the-nephilim.

33. What is hell? Is it a real place? Where is it?

1. "Sheol," *New World Encyclopedia*, 2008, www.newworldencyclopedia.org/entry/Sheol.

2. Timothy R. Phillips, "Hades," in *Baker's Evangelical Dictionary of Biblical Theology* (Grand Rapids, MI: Baker, 1996), www.biblestudytools.com/dictionary/hades/.

3. "Gehenna," *New World Encyclopedia*, 2013, www.newworldencyclopedia.org/entry/Gehenna.

34. Do Satan and the demons torment people in hell?

1. Bill Wiese, *23 Minutes in Hell* (Lake Mary, FL: Charisma House, 2006). Video available at www.youtube.com/watch?v=AYxKRoONrfY.

35. Do those in hell really burn forever?

1. Graeme Loftus, "Apocalypse: the Millennium and the End of Sin," Seventh-Day Adventist Church, June 2010, www.adventist.org/en/beliefs/apocalypse/the-millennium-and-the-end-of-sin/article/go/0/the-millenium-and-the-end-of-sin and "Beliefs: Apocalypse," Seventh-Day Adventist Church, www.adventist.org/en/beliefs/apocalypse.
2. See, for example, Clark H. Pinnock, "The Destruction of the Finally Impenitent," *Criswell Theological Review:* 4.2 (1990), 243–259, www.truthaccordingtoscripture.com/documents/death/destruction-of-the-finally-impenitent.php#.U1wjAaJWiSo.
3. Rob Bell, *Love Wins: A Book About Heaven, Hell, and the Fate of Every Person Who Ever Lived* (New York: HarperCollins, 2011).

38. Who will win the spiritual war between God and Satan?

1. Howard Robinson, "Dualism," *Stanford Encyclopedia of Philosophy*, November 3, 2011, http://plato.stanford.edu/entries/dualism/.
2. G.F. Handel, "Hallelujah Chorus," *Messiah*, 1741, http://www.hallelujah-chorus.com/text/english.html.

39. What is Satan's plan of attack on the human race?

1. Martin Luther, "A Mighty Fortress Is Our God," 1529, translated by Frederic H. Hedge, 1853, www.cyberhymnal.org/htm/m/i/mightyfo.htm.

41. Does Satan rule over the world today?

1. Martin Luther, "A Mighty Fortress Is Our God," 1529, translated by Frederic H. Hedge, 1853, www.cyberhymnal.org/htm/m/i/mightyfo.htm.
2. Thayer and Smith, "Greek Lexicon entry for *exousia*," *The NAS New Testament Greek Lexicon*, 1999, www.biblestudytools.com/lexicons/greek/nas/exousia.html.

42. What is the occult? Does Satan have anything to do with the occult?

1. "Who Do Witches Worship?" *Witchway*, www.witchway.net/wicca/faq.html.
2. *Manifest Creation*, www.rajunasrefuge.com/creation.html.
3. *Satan's Heaven*, www.satansheaven.com.
4. "Do Witches Worship Satan?" "Is Wicca Related to Satanism?" *Witchway*, www.witchway.net/wicca/faq.html.

44. Are there really people who worship Satan?

1. Ken Ammi, "Is Miranda Barbour a Satanist, and Are Her Murders Satanic Crimes?" *Examiner.com*, www.examiner.com/article/is-miranda-barbour-a-satanist-and-are-her-murders-satanic-crimes.

2. B.A. Robinson, "The Church of Satan (CoS): Quotes, Overview, Founding, Beliefs," *Ontario Consultants on Religious Tolerance*, 2006. Retrieved on March 30, 2014, at http://www.religioustolerance.org/satanis1.htm.

3. Sean Thomas, "The Devil Worshippers of Iraq," *The Telegraph*, August 19, 2007, www.telegraph.co.uk/news/worldnews/1560714/The-Devil-worshippers-of-Iraq.html.

46. Is fortune-telling (divination) demonic?

1. *"Echousan pneuma puthonos,"* Greek Interlinear Bible, www.scripture4all.org/OnlineInterlinear/NTpdf/act16.pdf.

2. "Python," *Encyclopedia Britannica*, www.britannica.com/EBchecked/topic/485283/Python.

47. Are witches real?

1. "Witch" *Merriam-Webster Dictionary*, www.merriam-webster.com/dictionary/witch.

2. For example, Genesis 41:8; Exodus 7:11; Deuteronomy 18:10 (NKJV); Daniel 1:20; Jeremiah 27:9.

3. Patti Wigington, "Basic Principles and Concepts of Wicca," *About.com*, http://paganwiccan.about.com/od/wiccaandpaganismbasics/p/Wiccan_Basics.htm.

4. Rebecca Beatrice Brooks, "The Salem Witch Trials," *History of Massachusetts*, August 28, 2011, http://historyofmassachusetts.org/the-salem-witch-trials.

48. Is Satan behind Halloween?

1. David Emery, "A Quick Guide to the Origin and History of Halloween," *About.com, Urban Legends*, http://urbanlegends.about.com/od/halloween/a/History-Of-Halloween.htm.

2. Travis Allen, "Christians and Halloween," *Grace to You*, www.gty.org/resources/articles/a123.

3. Robert Rothwell, "What Is Reformation Day All About?" Ligonier Ministries, October 30, 2013, www.ligonier.org/blog/what-reformation-day-all-about.

49. Is a séance demonic? Should we try to contact the dead?

1. B. A. Robinson, "New Age Spirituality," *Ontario Consultants on Religious Tolerance*, 2011, www.religioustolerance.org/newage.htm.

2. "Channeling," *Channeling.net*, http://channeling.net/.

Mark H. Muska is Associate Professor of Biblical and Theological Studies at the University of Northwestern St. Paul. Dr. Muska received his EdD from St. Mary's University and his ThM from Dallas Theological Seminary. He is a regular guest on "Ask the Professor," fielding live calls from listeners on the KTIS AM *Connecting Faith* program. He lives with his family near St. Paul, Minnesota.

More Bible-Based Resources

The Bible is filled with answers to your questions about heaven, explaining what it looks like, who will be there, and how to get there in the first place. Here you will find clear explanations of these passages, and get an honest and beautiful picture of our eternal home.

50 Things You Need to Know About Heaven
by Dr. John Hart

Angels and demons fascinate us because they are surrounded by mystery. This book includes every Scripture passage relating to these beings along with brief commentaries to help you develop a biblical point of view. These answers, taken straight from God's Word, will quench your curiosity about angels and rest your fears about demons.

Everything the Bible Says About Angels and Demons
Visit bethanyhouse.com for a list of other topics covered in this series.

BETHANYHOUSE

Stay up-to-date on your favorite books and authors with our free e-newsletters. Sign up today at bethanyhouse.com.

Find us on Facebook. facebook.com/BHPnonfiction

Follow us on Twitter. @bethany_house